diet for a
HAPPY HEART

By Jeanne Jones

Preface by Max Ellenberg, M.D.
Drawings by Jeremiah

101 Productions
San Francisco
1975

FOR BOB, TOM AND DAVID
THEIR VERY OWN COOKBOOK!

In Grateful Acknowledgement:
Taita Pearn, M.S., R.D., for technical research and consulting.
Effie Jackson for assistance in recipe preparation and testing.
Cora King for manuscript preparation.
Robert E. Harris for culinary consulting.
Hubert Latimer for introducing me to Jeremiah Goodman.

Second Printing, May, 1976
Copyright © 1975 by Jeanne Jones
Drawings copyright © 1975 by Jeremiah Goodman

Printed in the United States of America

Published by 101 Productions
834 Mission Street, San Francisco, California 94103

Distributed to the book trade in the United States by
Charles Scribner's Sons, New York, and in Canada
by Van Nostrand Reinhold Ltd., Toronto

Library of Congress Cataloging in Publication Data

Jones, Jeanne.
    Diet for a happy heart.

    Bibliography: p.
    Includes index.
    1. Cookery for cardiacs.   2. Heart—Diseases—
Prevention.   I. Title.
RM221.C3J66   641.5'63   75-6713
ISBN 0-912238-58-5
ISBN 0-912238-57-7 pbk.

contents

preface

Heart attacks due to coronary artery disease constitute one of our greatest health problems. They are associated with a high mortality rate and prolonged disability. Therefore, it is mandatory that we avail ourselves of all measures that offer protection against their occurrence. At the present time, one of the most readily available, most reliable and most rewarding approaches is diet. The constitution of this diet is based on three fundamental features that play a definite role in this disease: sugar, fats and total calories.

SUGAR An amazing number of all heart attacks in this country is related to diabetes! This startling and highly significant fact has been demonstrated by studies that show an overwhelmingly high (up to 70 percent) incidence of abnormal carbohydrate (sugar) metabolism in this group of patients. Since heart attacks are so common in diabetes, this deviation points to a predisposition to coronary artery disease. It indicates that most individuals with vascular disease are unrecognized mild or latent diabetics in whom the arteriosclerosis (hardening of arteries) overshadows the carbohydrate disturbance. Conversely, the presence of arteriosclerosis makes highly likely the associated presence of diabetes and this dictates the appropriate therapeutic dietary approach—specifically, refined sugars and sweets are contraindicated, and carbohydrates must be regulated in the coronary diet.

Another fascinating fact is worthy of mention. There is a sharp increase in diabetes and coronary artery disease among many ethnic groups who, after geographical translocation, have adopted a "Western diet." This includes a sharp increase in carbohydrates and especially in refined carbohydrates. In other words, the continued use of excess sugar, *per se,* is deleterious and may precipitate diabetes as well as coronary artery disease.

FATS This very important component plays a fundamental role in determining the effects of the diet. It is now universally recognized and accepted that blood lipids (this includes cholesterol, triglycerides, etc.) influence the degree of arteriosclerosis. Not only must we consider the quantity of fats, but we must also carefully calculate their quality, with emphasis on polyunsaturated fats rather than the saturated variety. Here, too, the influence of elevated blood sugar is apparent. Not only are lipids more often elevated in the diabetic, but patients with high blood fats tend to have glucose intolerance. In addition, some types of hyperlipidemia are aggravated by high carbohydrate diets as well as by the refined sugars.

4

CALORIES Obesity is the oldest recognized factor associated with heart disease. Life insurance statistics have pointed out this association for a great many years. Obesity, which is so common in diabetes, is a common denominator for increased fats and impaired glucose tolerance (diabetes). The association of coronary artery disease with elevation of blood lipids, abnormal glucose tolerance and obesity is established.

The gist of all the foregoing is to point out and emphasize the overriding implications of the interplay between diabetes, hyperlipidemia and obesity that results in hardening of the arteries. Since these factors are conditioned by carbohydrates—especially refined sugars, fats—especially saturated fats and total calories, the conclusion is evident: The dietary attack must be multi-pronged and not simplistically confined to one aspect such as cholesterol. Fortunately, this is one of the few readily available areas where preventive aspects for this very common and serious disease can be applied, and prevention is the ideal goal.

This comprehensive guide by Jeanne Jones—the Calculating Cook—is admirably suited to help prevent coronary artery disease, the scourge of modern civilization. The author presents, for the first time, a book that recognizes and encompasses the intimate interrelationship and interdependence between diabetes, fats and obesity. At this stage of our knowledge, this thrust offers one of the best and most readily available deterrents and preventives of coronary artery disease. Written in an exciting, readable and practical fashion, this book is indeed an incentive to accept such proffered help with welcome arms, understanding and cooperation.

MAX ELLENBERG, M.D.
Clinical Professor of Medicine, Mount Sinai School of Medicine
Attending Physician for Diabetes, Mount Sinai Hospital
President, American Diabetes Association, Inc., 1974-1975
New York City, New York
April 23, 1974

introduction

After my recent book, *The Calculating Cook,* was published, I immediately started receiving many requests from both friends and doctors to do another cookbook. Most of the requests favored a book for coronary diets, low in cholesterol and low in saturated fats.

Although there are many such books on the market today, none of them includes a diet which is also sugar-free. More and more experts in the field agree that a sugar-free diet is as important to the coronary patient as it is to the diabetic or dieter.

I had already given thought to writing this book, when one day my husband dashed into the house, happily handing me the latest cholesterol report from his doctor. In the six months we had been married, his cholesterol count had come down from a dangerously high level to well within normal limits! He was so proud of himself that he reminded me of a little boy coming home from school with a 'straight A' report card for the first time. *And I* was so proud of myself, I started writing this book the very next day!

I realized I had been keeping him so satisfied with the foods he *should* be eating, that he did not have the time nor appetite left for eating the things he *should not* eat. This encouraged me to help other people on restricted diets to prepare gourmet-type meals which would be so tasteful to them that they would not miss the fried eggs, buttered bread, giant steaks and rich, calorie-packed desserts that had gotten them into all the trouble in the first place.

The basic purpose of this book is to give you delicious, interesting recipes for a *Happy Heart* diet. Dieters and diabetics will find this book equally useful. It is actually, in many ways, a sequel to my first book, *The Calculating Cook.*

I have again based the menus on the Diabetic Diet program because it is the most frequently prescribed diet for health problems when used at the correct calorie level with the necessary dietary restrictions included in it. It is simply a perfectly balanced, sugar-free diet, applicable to all calorie levels. Many famous health spas use this diet. The well-known, highly successful Weight Watchers Program is largely based on it.

I have made every recipe in this book a sufficient number of times in my own kitchen so that I can assure you of success in making each recipe yourself. I must admit it sometimes took me many months to get a particular dish seasoned to my own satisfaction before I included the recipe in this book.

At the end of *Happy Heart* you will find two one-week sample menus at two different calorie levels. Each menu also limits the amount of cholesterol to 200 milligrams per day.

There are no saturated oils nor sugar in any recipe in this book!

Not only will a sugar-free diet aid greatly in controlling weight, but your dentist will love you for "kicking the sweet-habit."

Okay! Read through the book, glance at the menus, make your first shopping list and go to the market. *Then* start taking off the pounds and lowering the cholesterol count!

happy heart diet program

Before we get into what you *should not eat,* let us get off to a more positive start and talk about what you *should eat!* I prefer to think of this approach as the *go*-food, *caution*-food and *stop*-food theory. You will be amazed to discover how many more *go* foods there are than *stop* foods! This, in itself, is a *positive* approach.

I feel that too little emphasis is placed on low-calorie cooking. Far too much time and importance are given to making high-calorie dishes which are low in saturated fats and cholesterol. Granted the latter is an important facet in a Happy Heart diet, but the very first thing most heart specialists tell most patients is "lose weight!"

Regardless of whether you are trying to lose weight or just maintain your present weight, the most important thing for your health and your heart is a well-balanced diet. Of course, you can lose weight on many of the so-called "fad diets." Many people have lost weight eating only apples and cheese three times a day, or only bananas and milk six times a day, or only eating meat and drinking water all day long. But, you will *not* get sufficient nutrients to properly maintain vital body functions on any of these semi-fasting diets. The only sensible way to lose weight and maintain your health at the same time is to *lower* the calorie intake in a perfectly balanced manner.

When speaking to teenage groups, I frequently use an easily understood graphic example to illustrate my point. I compare the human body to an expensive racing car such as a Ferrari. I tell them that you would not invest in a Ferrari and then run its highly tuned racing engine on the least expensive, low-octane gasoline you could find. Your own body is also a very complex, highly tuned machine. When you run it on "junk foods" that do not provide the vitamins and minerals necessary for proper growth and maintenance, it will not perform at its best. It may even develop serious problems.

Treat your body to a perfectly balanced diet and it will not only function better, but you will quickly notice other improvements. Your skin will look better, your hair will be shinier, your eyes will be brighter *and* even your disposition will improve!

happy heart diet program

We talk a lot about cholesterol. Therefore, I think it is important to know *what* it is, *where* it comes from, and *why* we should control it. How can we control it?

Cholesterol is a waxy material present in foods of animal origin, such as egg yolk, meat and animal fat. It is also found in animal products such as cream, butter and some cheese, as well as shellfish and organ meats of all animals.

A limited amount of cholesterol is necessary for good health. When the body has too much of it, cholesterol slowly builds up in the arteries to roughen, narrow and reduce the size of the vessels through which blood must flow. This build-up along the artery walls is called atherosclerosis. If enough cholesterol and other plaque material build up to actually interfere with the flow of blood in the coronary arteries, a heart attack or stroke is the result.

We *can* control the build-up of cholesterol. We can do it in several ways. Here's how: First and most obvious, cut down on the amount of foods containing cholesterol. Limit the intake of saturated fats, such as animal fats, coconut oil and hydrogenated vegetable fats which help the cholesterol build-up. Although saturated fats do not contain cholesterol, they tend to help build up cholesterol in the blood vessels. Monounsaturated fats, such as olive oil and peanut oil stand on neutral ground because they neither help nor hurt us. They do not cause cholesterol build-up, but neither do they rid the artery walls of cholesterol already deposited. They contain the same number of calories as polyunsaturated fats. Therefore, if you are on a low-calorie diet, it is best to limit the intake of monounsaturated fats in favor of the polyunsaturates.

Polyunsaturated fats are the good guys. They include such oils as safflower, corn and cottonseed oil. Sesame and sunflower seed oils are also acceptable. Many doctors feel that they tend to help rid the artery walls of newly deposited cholesterol and thereby enlarge the blood vessels and reduce the cholesterol problem to some extent. For this reason, I think in a low calorie diet a greater proportion of the fats should be in the polyunsaturated category.

It also has been stated by prominent doctors that there is often a definite correlation between high carbohydrate intake and high cholesterol levels. Many experts agree that, in order to lower the blood lipids (including cholesterol and triglycerides), it is usually necessary to lower the carbohydrate intake.

Sugar is not essential for the body to function properly. An adequate amount of carbohydrates is obtained from fruits, starches and many vegetables in a well-balanced diet. Therefore, why waste calories on something we do not need? Also, sugar is not allowed in the diabetic diet; diabetes is one of the major causes of heart attacks and all other vascular diseases.

In most cases, high cholesterol counts can be lowered by proper diet. It's not too late to start aiming toward a Happy Heart!

Remember the old saying: "An ounce of prevention is worth a pound of cure." Even before a child is born, good nutrition is an important factor in proper development. Babies should not be given diets high in saturated fats and refined sugar. Start training small children in good eating habits. Coronary build-up can start in childhood, so apply basically the same rules and diet principles to children that you apply to adults when controlling the amounts of cholesterol, saturated fats and sugar. *Then* you will, indeed, be raising a Happy Heart and teaching good lifelong habits.

GOOD RULES

For keeping the polyunsaturated fats *up* and the saturated fats *down!*

• Eliminate whole milk from your shopping list. Use low-fat milk, non-fat milk or buttermilk. When cooking with milk lower in fat, it will take you longer to thicken sauces, so be patient!
• Get into the habit of using egg substitutes. Eggs should be limited to two or three times per week.
• Beef, lamb, pork and ham should be limited to three meals per week, and each serving to three ounces.
• The remaining 11 main meals should include protein, such as poultry, fish, veal, low-fat cheeses, egg substitute and meat substitutes.
• Dried beans, peanut butter and nuts are also good sources of protein.
• Use polyunsaturated margarine instead of butter.

In my recipes, I *specifically* call for corn oil margarine. Pure corn oil margarine is considered by doctors to be better for your health than some of the other mixed oil margarines; it also has a better flavor when heated. Use polyunsaturated oils for salad dressings and for cooking. I always specify corn oil because I prefer the taste and texture over safflower oil and it is practically as low in polyunsaturated fats. I also specify safflower oil mayonnaise in my recipes because it is the mayonnaise lowest in saturated fats.

FOOD GROUPS AND CHARTS

Although I am using the Diabetic Exchange Diet for the diet program in *Diet for a Happy Heart,* I have made three changes in terminology, which seem to be more easily understood by everyone.
First, the term "exchange" is changed to "portion." *Second,* the food group usually called "bread exchange" is titled "starches" which better describes the entire food group. *Third,* the food group usually called "meat exchange" is titled "proteins," again because it better describes the entire category listed as "protein portion."
The diet is to be used in exactly the same way the Exchange Diet is used. Your doctor tells you how many portions of *each* food group you may have *each* day. You then may choose from each food group the portion you wish for the meals during that day. The variety is practically endless! All that is important is that you have the proper number of portions from *each* food group *each* day.

happy heart diet program

FRUITS

Each portion below equals:
1 fruit portion
Contains approximately:
10 grams carbohydrate
40 calories

mg. chol. = milligrams cholesterol

mg. chol.	FRUIT/PORTION
0	Apple: 1 2 inches in diameter
0	Apple juice: 1/2 cup
0	Applesauce, unsweetened: 1/2 cup
0	Apricots, fresh: 2 medium**
0	Apricots, dried: 3 halves**
0	Avocado: see Fats list
0	Banana: 1/2 small
0	Berries (blackberries, raspberries, strawberries): 1 cup
0	Blueberries: 2/3 cup
0	Cantaloupe: 1/4 6 inches in diameter***
0	Cherries, sweet: 10 large
0	Crenshaw melon: 2-inch wedge
0	Dates: 2
0	Figs, fresh: 1 large
0	Figs, dried: 1 large
0	Grapefruit: 1/2 4 inches in diameter*
0	Grapefruit juice: 1/2 cup*
0	Grapes: 12 large
0	Grapes, Thompson seedless: 40 or 1 cup
0	Grape juice: 1/4 cup
0	Guava: 2/3*

mg. chol.	FRUIT/PORTION
0	Honeydew melon: 1/4 5 inches in diameter
0	Kumquats: 3
0	Lemon juice: 1/2 cup
0	Lime juice: 1/2 cup
0	Loquats: 3
0	Lychees, fresh: 4
0	Mango: 1/2 small**
0	Mountain apples: 2 medium
0	Nectarine: 1 medium
0	Orange: 1 small*
0	Orange juice: 1/2 cup*
0	Papaya: 1/3 medium*
0	Passion fruit: 1
0	Passion fruit juice: 1/3 cup
0	Peach: 1 medium
0	Pear: 1 small
0	Persimmon: 1/2 medium
0	Pineapple, fresh or canned without sugar: 1/2 cup
0	Pineapple juice: 1/3 cup
0	Plums: 2 medium
0	Pomegranate: 1 small
0	Prunes, fresh or dried: 2
0	Prune juice: 1/4 cup
0	Raisins: 2 tablespoons
0	Tangerines: 1 large or 2 small
0	Tomato catsup: 3 tablespoons
0	Watermelon: 3/4 cup

GROUP B VEGETABLES

Each portion below equals:
1 group B vegetable portion
   (cooked or raw)
Contains approximately:
7 grams carbohydrate
2 grams protein
36 calories

mg. chol. = milligrams cholesterol

mg. chol.	VEGETABLE/PORTION
0	Artichoke, whole, base and ends of leaves: 1
0	Beets: 1/2 cup
0	Carrots, medium: 1**
0	Celery root: 1/2 cup
0	Green beans, mature: 1/2 cup
0	Jerusalem artichokes: 1/2 cup
0	Lima beans, baby: 1/4 cup
0	Onions: 1/2 cup
0	Parsnips, small: 1
0	Peas: 1/2 cup
0	Pumpkin: 1/2 cup*
0	Rutabagas: 1/2 cup
0	Squash, acorn: 1/2 cup
0	Squash, hubbard: 1/2 cup
0	Tomato catsup: 1-1/2 tablespoons
0	Tomato paste: 3 tablespoons
0	Tomato sauce: 1/2 cup
0	Turnips: 1/2 cup
0	V-8 juice: 2/3 cup**

*   good source of vitamin C
**   good source of vitamin A
*** good source of vitamins A and C

happy heart diet program

STARCHES

Each portion below equals:
1 starch portion
Contains approximately:
15 grams carbohydrate
2 grams protein
68 calories

$\frac{mg.}{chol.}$ = milligrams cholesterol

√	very low in saturated fats
√√	low in saturated fats
√√√	high in saturated fats

mg. chol.	VEGETABLES/PORTION
0	Beans, dry or cooked (lima, navy, kidney): 1/2 cup
0	Beans, baked, without pork: 1/4 cup
0	Corn, on-the-cob: 1 4 inches long
0	Corn, cooked and drained: 1/3 cup
0	Hominy: 1/2 cup
0	Lentils, dried, cooked: 1/2 cup
0	Parsnips: 2/3 cup
0	Peas, dry, cooked, black-eyed, split: 1/2 cup
0	Poi: 1/2 cup
0	Potatoes, sweet, yams: 1/4 cup**
0	Potatoes, white, baked or boiled: 1 2 inches in diameter
0	Potatoes, white, mashed: 1/2 cup
0	Potato chips: 15 2 inches in diameter √√√
0	Pumpkin, canned: 1 cup
0	Rice, cooked: 1/2 cup
0	Tomato catsup, commercial: 3 tablespoons

** good source of vitamin A

13

happy heart diet program

mg. chol.	BREADS/PORTION
0	Bagel: 1/2
0	Biscuit (omit 1 fat portion):
0	1 2 inches in diameter
0	Bread (white, wheat, rye and
0	sourdough): 1 slice
0	Breadsticks: 4 9 inches long
0	Bun, hamburger: 1/2
0	Bun, hot dog: 2/3
0	Corn bread: 1 piece
0	1-1/2 inches square
0	Cracked wheat (bulgar):
0	2 tablespoons
0	Croutons, plain: 1/2 cup
0	English muffin: 1/2
0	Melba toast: 6 slices
0	Muffins, unsweetened:
0	1 2 inches in diameter
0	Matzo cracker, plain:
0	1 6 inches in diameter
0	Pancakes: 2 3 inches in
0	diameter
0	Popover: 1
0	Roll: 1 2 inches in diameter
0	Rusks: 2
0	Spoon bread: 1/2 cup
0	Tortilla, corn, flour:
0	1 7 inches in diameter
0	Waffle: 1 4 inches in diameter

mg. chol.	CEREALS/PORTION
0	All-Bran: 1/3 cup
0	Bran Flakes: 1/2 cup
0	Cheerios: 1 cup
0	Concentrate (add 1 protein
0	portion): 1/4 cup
0	Corn flakes: 2/3 cup
0	Cornmeal, cooked: 1/2 cup

mg. chol.	CEREALS/PORTION
0	Cream-of-Wheat, cooked:
0	1/2 cup
0	Grapenuts: 1/4 cup
0	Grapenut Flakes: 1/2 cup
0	Grits, cooked: 1/2 cup
0	Kix: 3/4 cup
0	Krumbles: 1/2 cup
0	Malt-O-Meal, cooked: 1/2 cup
0	Maypo, cooked: 1/2 cup
0	Matzo meal, cooked: 1/2 cup
0	Oatmeal, cooked: 1/2 cup
0	Puffed rice: 1-1/2 cups
0	Puffed wheat: 1-1/2 cups
0	Rice Krispies: 2/3 cup
0	Shredded wheat, biscuit:
0	1 large
0	Special K: 1-1/4 cups
0	Wheat Chex: 1 cup
0	Steel cut oats, cooked: 1/2 cup
0	Rice, cooked: 1/2 cup
9.4	Wheat germ, defatted (omit
3.1	1 fat portion): 1 ounce or
	3 tablespoons
0	Wheaties: 2/3 cup

mg. chol.	CRACKERS/PORTION
0	Animal: 8
0	Arrowroot: 3
0	Cheese tidbits: 3/4 cup ✓✓✓
0	Graham: 2
0	Oyster: 20 or 1/2 cup
0	Pretzels: 10 very thin, or
0	1 large
0	Saltines: 5
0	Soda: 3
0	Ritz: 6 ✓✓✓
0	Rye Crisp: 3
0	Rye thins: 10

mg. chol.	CRACKERS/PORTION
0	Triangle thins: 14 ✓✓✓
0	Triscuits: 5 ✓✓✓
0	Vegetable thins: 12 ✓✓
0	Wheat thins: 12 ✓✓✓

mg. chol.	FLOURS/PORTION
	Arrowroot: 2 tablespoons
	All-purpose: 2-1/2 tablespoons
	Bisquick: 1-1/2 tablespoons ✓✓✓
	Bran: 5 tablespoons
	Buckwheat: 3 tablespoons
	Cake: 2-1/2 tablespoons
	Cornmeal: 3 tablespoons
	Cornstarch: 2 tablespoons
	Matzo meal: 3 tablespoons
	Potato flour: 2-1/2 tablespoons
	Rye, light: 4 tablespoons
	Whole wheat: 3 tablespoons
	Noodles, macaroni, spaghetti,
	cooked: 1/2 cup
	Noodles, dry, egg: 3-1/2 ounces
	Noodles, cooked, egg:
	3-1/2 ounces

mg. chol.	MISCELLANEOUS/PORTION
0	Cocoa, dry, unsweetened:
	2-1/2 tablespoons
26.3	Ice cream, low-saturated (add
	2 fat portions): 1/2 cup
7.7	Happy Heart Ice Cream:
	1/2 cup
0	Popcorn, popped, unbuttered:
	1-1/2 cups
0	Potato chips, Fritos
	(add 2 fat portions):
	3/4 ounce or 1/2 cup
0	Sponge cake, plain: 1-1/2-inch
	cube

PROTEINS

Each portion below equals:
1 ounce (unless otherwise specified), 1 cube 1 x 1 x 1 inches or 1 standard slice 3-1/2 x 3-1/2 x 1/8 inches and 1 protein portion

Contains approximately:
7 grams protein
5 grams fat
73 calories

mg. chol. = milligrams cholesterol

√	very low in saturated fats
√√	low in saturated fats
√√√	high in saturated fats
†	cholesterol figure not available
††	depends on brand

CHEESE/PORTION

mg. chol.	CHEESE/PORTION
28.4	American: 1 ounce √
21.16	Bleu: 1 ounce or 1/4 cup, crumbled √√
30.1	Cheddar: 1 ounce √√
8.4	Cottage cheese, creamed: 1/4 cup √
2.6	Cottage cheese, low-fat: 1/4 cup √
29.1	Edam: 1 ounce √√√
3	Farmer: 1/4 cup, crumbled √
16	Feta: 1 ounce √
3	Hoop: 1/4 cup √
21	Liederkranz: 1 ounce √√√
18	Monterey Jack: 1 ounce √√√
17.4	Mozzarella: 1 ounce √√√
25	Muenster: 1 ounce √√√
14.8	Parmesan: 1/4 cup, 2/3 ounce or 4 tablespoons √√

CHEESE/PORTION

mg. chol.	CHEESE/PORTION
18.2	Pimiento cheese spread (omit 1 fat portion): 1 ounce √√√
3	Pot cheese: 1/4 cup √
29.1	Ricotta, regular: 1/4 cup or 2 ounces √√
18.2	Ricotta, part skim: 1/4 cup or 2 ounces √√
14.8	Romano: 1/4 cup, 2/3 ounce or 4 tablespoons √√
24	Roquefort: 1 ounce or 1/4 cup, crumbled √√√
21	Stilton: 1 ounce or 1/4 cup, crumbled √√√
28	Swiss: 1 ounce √√√

EGGS AND EGG SUBSTITUTES/PORTION

mg. chol.	EGGS AND EGG SUBSTITUTES/PORTION
252	Eggs, medium: 1
0	Liquid egg substitute: 1/4 cup
0	Dry egg substitute: 3 tablespoons

COLD CUTS/PORTION

mg. chol.	COLD CUTS/PORTION
25.9	Bologna: 1 ounce or 1 slice 4-1/2 inches in diameter, 1/8 inch thick √√√
†	Liverwurst: 1 slice 3 inches in diameter, 1/4 inch thick
25.9	Spam: 1 ounce √√√
25.9	Salami (add 1 fat portion): 1 ounce or 1 slice 4 inches in diameter, 1/3 inch thick √√
25.9	Vienna sausage: 2-1/2 sausages or 1 ounce √√√

CHICKEN/PORTION

mg. chol.	CHICKEN/PORTION
25.8	Broiled or roasted: 1 ounce or 1 slice 3 x 2 x 1/8 inches
22.4	Breast, without skin: 1/2 small, 1 ounce or 1/4 cup, chopped
†	Heart: 1 ounce
25.8	Leg: 1/2 medium or 1 ounce
211.4	Liver: 1 medium or 1 ounce

DUCK/PORTION

mg. chol.	DUCK/PORTION
†	Roasted, without skin: 1 ounce or 1 slice 3 x 2 x 1/8 inches
†	Wild duck, without skin: 1/4 small

TURKEY/PORTION

mg. chol.	TURKEY/PORTION
22.4	Meat, without skin: 1 ounce or 1 slice 3 x 2 x 1/8 inches

OTHER POULTRY AND GAME/PORTION

mg. chol.	OTHER POULTRY AND GAME/PORTION
30	Buffalo: 1 ounce or 1 slice 3 x 2 x 1/8 inches
†	Cornish game hen, without skin: 1/4 bird or 1 ounce
†	Pheasant: 1-1/2 ounces
25.8	Rabbit: 1 ounce or 1 slice 3 x 2 x 1/8 inches
†	Quail, without skin: 1/4 bird or 1 ounce
†	Squab, without skin: 1/4 bird or 1 ounce
†	Venison, lean, roast or steak: 1 ounce or 1 slice 3 x 2 x 1/8 inches

happy heart diet program

FISH AND SEAFOOD/PORTION

mg. chol.	
24.4	Abalone: 1-1/3 ounces ✓
18.3	Albacore, canned in oil: 1 ounce
21.4	Anchovy fillets: 9
27.1	Bass: 1-1/2 ounces
85.7	Caviar: 1 ounce
18	Clams, fresh: 3 large or 1-1/2 ounces ✓
27	Clams, canned: 1-1/2 ounces ✓
†	Clam juice: 1-1/2 cups
18.1	Cod: 1 ounce
43	Crab, canned: 1/2 ounce ✓
42.5	Crab, cracked, fresh: 1-1/2 ounces ✓
30.2	Flounder: 1-2/3 ounces
55	Frog legs: 2 large or 3 ounces
18.1	Halibut: 1 ounce or 1 piece 2 x 2 x 1 inches
27	Herring, pickled: 1-1/4 ounces
31	Lobster, fresh: 1-1/2 ounces, 1/4 cup or 1/4 small lobster ✓
36	Lobster, canned: 1-1/2 ounces ✓
23	Oysters, fresh: 3 medium or 1-1/2 ounces
25.5	Oysters, canned: 1-1/2 ounces
27.1	Perch: 1-1/2 ounces
27.1	Red snapper: 1-1/2 ounces
18.4	Salmon: 1 ounce
16	Salmon, canned: 1-1/2 ounces
24.4	Sand dabs: 1-1/2 ounces
40	Sardines: 4 small
23	Scallops: 3 medium or 1-1/2 ounces
30	Sole: 1-2/3 ounces
48	Shrimp, fresh: 5 medium ✓

FISH/PORTION

mg. chol.	
64	Shrimp, canned: 5 medium or 1-1/2 ounces ✓
27.1	Swordfish: 1-1/2 ounces ✓
27.1	Trout: 1-1/2 ounces
18.1	Tuna: 1 ounce
36.7	Tuna, canned: 1/4 cup
27.1	Turbot: 1-1/2 ounces

BEEF/PORTION

mg. chol.	
571.4	Brains: 1 ounce
31.3	Brisket: 1 ounce
26	Corned beef, canned: 1 ounce or 1 slice 3 x 2 x 1/8 inches
41.8	Flank steak: 1-1/3 ounces ✓
25.9	Frankfurters: 1/2 pound (8 to 9 per pound) ✓✓✓
42.8	Heart: 1 ounce or 1 slice 3 x 2 x 1/8 inches ✓
30.3	Hamburger, very lean (4 ounces raw = 3 ounces cooked): 1 ounce
107.1	Kidney: 1 ounce or 1 slice 3 x 2 x 1/8 inches
124.1	Liver: 1 ounce or 1 slice 2 x 3 x 1/8 inches
31.3	Rib roast: 1 ounce, 1/4 cup, chopped, or 1 slice 2 x 3 x 1/8 inches
31.3	Short ribs, very lean: 1 rib or 1 ounce
30	Steak, very lean (filet mignon, New York, sirloin, T-bone): 1 ounce or 1 slice 3 x 2 x 1/8 inches
†	Tongue: 1 slice 3 x 2 x 1/4 inches ✓
†	Tripe: 1 ounce or 1 piece 5 x 2 inches ✓

LAMB/PORTION

mg. chol.	
28	Chops: 1/2 small chop or 1 ounce
27.7	Roast: 1 ounce, 1 slice 3 x 2 x 1/8 inches or 1/4 cup, chopped

PEANUT BUTTER/PORTION

mg. chol.	
0	Peanut butter: 2 tablespoons

PORK/PORTION

mg. chol.	
4.5	Bacon (see Fats): 1 slice ✓✓✓
25.3	Canadian bacon: 1 slice 2-1/2 inches in diameter, 1/4 inch thick
25	Chops: 1/2 small chop or 1 ounce
25.3	Ham: 1 ounce or 1 slice 3 x 2 x 1/8 inches
124.1	Liver: 1 ounce
25	Roast, lean: 1 ounce, 1 slice 3 x 2 x 1/8 inches or 1/4 cup, chopped
25.9	Sausage: 2 small or 1 ounce ✓✓✓
25.3	Spareribs, without fat: meat from 3 medium or 1 ounce ✓✓✓

VEAL/PORTION

mg. chol.	
28.7	Chop: 1/2 small or 1 ounce
29	Cutlet: 1 ounce or 1 slice 3 x 2 x 1/8 inches
	Calves' liver: 1 ounce or 1 slice 3 x 2 x 1/8 inches
28.7	Roast: 1 ounce or 1 slice 3 x 2 x 1/8 inches
71.4	Sweetbreads: 1 ounce, 1/4 pair or 1/4 cup, chopped

MILK

Each portion below equals:
1 milk portion
Contains approximately:
12 grams carbohydrate
8 grams protein
10 grams fat
170 calories

$\frac{mg.}{chol.}$ = milligrams cholesterol

$\frac{mg.}{chol.}$	ITEM/PORTION
32.7	Milk, whole: 1 cup
15.5	Milk, low-fat, 2% fat: 1 cup**
2.3	Milk, skim, non-fat: 1 cup*
1.7	Milk, powdered, skim: 1/4 cup*
32.7	Milk, evaporated, whole: 1/2 cup
2.3	Milk, evaporated, skim: 1/2 cup
7.8	Buttermilk: 1 cup*
17	Yogurt, plain, low-fat: 1 cup**
26	Ice milk: 1 cup

*   Add 2 fat portions to your menu if milk is non-fat.

** Add 1 fat portion to your menu if milk is low-fat.

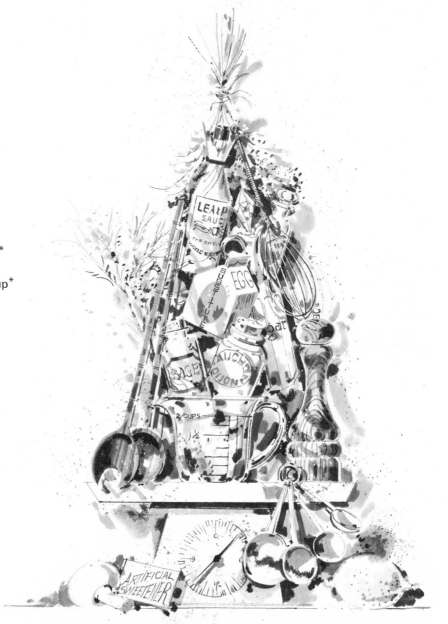

happy heart diet program

FATS

Each portion below equals:
1 fat portion
Contains approximately:
5 grams fat
45 calories

$\frac{mg.}{chol.}$ = milligrams cholesterol

✓	very low in saturated fats
✓✓	low in saturated fats
✓✓✓	high in saturated fats

| † | cholesterol figure not available |
| †† | depends on brand and ingredients |

ITEM/PORTION

ITEM/PORTION	mg. chol.
Avocado: 1/8 4 inches in diameter	0
Bacon, crisp: 1 slice ✓✓✓	7
Butter: 1 teaspoon ✓✓✓	12
Chocolate, bitter: 1/3 ounce or 1/3 square ✓✓✓	0
Cream cheese: 1 tablespoon	10
Cream, light, coffee: 2 tablespoons ✓✓✓	20
Cream, heavy, whipping: 1 tablespoon ✓✓✓	20
Cream, half-and-half: 3 tablespoons ✓✓✓	17
Cream, sour: 2 tablespoons ✓✓✓	16
Cream, sour, imitation: 2 tablespoons (Imo ✓✓✓, Matey ✓)	0
Margarine, polyunsaturated: 1 teaspoon	0
Mayonnaise: 1 teaspoon	2.6
Oils, polyunsaturated: 1 teaspoon	0
Olives: 5 small	0
Salad dressings, commercial	††
French oil and vinegar: 1-1/2 teaspoons	
Roquefort: 1 teaspoon	
Thousand Island (egg-free): 1 teaspoon	
Sauces, commercial	††
Béarnaise: 1 teaspoon	
Hollandaise: 1 teaspoon	
Tartar sauce: 1 teaspoon	
Sesame seeds: 2 teaspoons	0
Sunflower seeds: 1-1/4 teaspoons	0

NUTS/PORTION

NUTS/PORTION	mg. chol.
Almonds: 7	0
Butternuts: 2	0
Brazil nuts: 2	0
Cashews: 7	0
Coconut, fresh: 1 piece 1x1x3/8 inches ✓✓✓	0
Coconut, shredded, unsweetened: 2 tablespoons ✓✓✓	0
Filberts: 5	0
Hazelnuts: 5	0
Hickory nuts: 7 small	0
Macadamia nuts: 2	0
Peanuts: 6*	0
Pecans: 6 halves	0
Pine nuts: 1 tablespoon	0
Pistachio nuts: 15	0
Soy nuts, toasted: 3 tablespoons*	0
Walnuts, black: 5 halves	0
Walnuts, California: 5 halves	0

* high in protein

GO FOODS

UNLIMITED

The following foods need not be measured because calories are negligible. An excess of many of them, however, is not good for you.

Coffee
Tea
Clear broth
Consommé and bouillon (fat free)
Lemon
Gelatin (unsweetened)
Rennet tablets
Cranberries (unsweetened)
Mustard
Mint
Pickles (without sugar)
Saccharin and other non-caloric
    sweeteners
Sugar-free soft drinks
Herbs
Spices
Extracts
Angostura bitters
Soy sauce
Vinegar
Group A vegetables, uncooked

GROUP A VEGETABLES

You may eat any amount of these vegetables, if they are *uncooked.* Cooking concentrates the food value of these vegetables and therefore when cooked, *1 cup equals 1 portion.* If you wish you may substitute a double serving of group A cooked (2 cups) for 1 serving of group B.

Alfalfa sprouts
Asparagus
Bean sprouts
Broccoli***
Brussels sprouts*
Cabbage*
Cauliflower
Celery
Chayote
Chicory**
Chilies
Cilantro
Chives***
Cucumbers
Cranberries
Eggplant
Escarole**
Greens**
    Beet greens
    Chard
    Collard*
    Dandelion greens
    Kale*
    Mustard, fresh*
    Poke
    Spinach
Green onion tops
Lettuce
Mushrooms
Okra
Palm heart
Parsley***
Peppers, green and red*
Radishes
Romaine lettuce
Rhubarb
String beans
Summer squash
Tomatoes
Tomato juice: 1/2 cup
Water chestnuts: 3 medium
Watercress**
Zucchini squash

   *good source of vitamin C
  **good source of vitamin A
***good source of vitamins A and C

CAUTION FOODS

Egg yolks
Products containing egg yolks, such as
    egg noodles, egg custard, et
    cetera.
Shellfish, such as oysters, clams,
    scallops, lobster, shrimp, crab.
Organ meats of all animals, such as
    liver, heart, kidney, sweetbreads
    and brains.
Ice milk

happy heart diet program

STOP FOODS

Sugar
Candy
Honey
Jam
Jelly
Marmalade
Syrups
Pie
Cake
Cookies
Pastries
Sweetened condensed milk
Soft drinks
Gum, sweetened with sugar
Beer, wine and other alcoholic
     beverages (except with the
     consent of your doctor)
Butter
Cream
Whole milk
Ice cream
Homogenized peanut butter
Coconut
Saturated oils
Animal fat
Creamed foods
Chocolate

ALCOHOLIC BEVERAGES

    Whether you are allowed alcoholic beverages in your diet is a question to be decided between your doctor and you. There is no question that weight loss/maintenance is simplified greatly by not drinking. Liquor of all types is high in calories.

    A good way to think of a cocktail, highball or glass of wine is to visualize the drink as a slice of bread with a pat of butter on it. This image helps me more to refrain from having another cocktail or glass of wine than anything else does.

    There is another problem with drinking on a restricted diet. Alcohol can lead to waiting too long before eating or eating too much or eating something forbidden on the diet. Most doctors, however, consider cooking with wines completely acceptable. Wine adds so little food value to each portion, and all the alcohol is cooked away before the food is eaten.

CALORIE AND CARBOHYDRATE ALCOHOLIC BEVERAGES CHART

Ale, mild, 8 oz. = 98 C*, 8 GC**
Beer, 8 oz. = 114 C, 11 GC
WINES
Champagne brut, 3 oz. = 75 C, 1 GC
Champagne, extra dry,
   3 oz. = 87 C, 4 GC

Dubonnet, 3 oz. = 96 C, 7 GC
Dry Marsala, 3 oz. = 162 C, 18 GC
Sweet Marsala, 3 oz. = 182 C, 23 GC
Muscatel, 4 oz. = 158 C, 14 GC
Port, 4 oz. = 158 C, 14 GC
Red wine, dry, 3 oz. = 69 C,
   under 1 GC
Sake, 3 oz. = 75 C, 6 GC
Sherry, domestic, 3½ oz. = 84 C, 5 GC
Dry vermouth, 3½ oz. = 105 C, 1 GC
Sweet vermouth, 3½ oz. = 167 C, 12 GC
White wine, dry, 3 oz. = 74 C,
   under 1 GC
LIQUEURS AND CORDIALS
Creme de Cacao, 1 oz. = 101 C, 12 GC
Creme de Menthe, 1 oz. = 112 C,
   13 GC
Curacao, 1 oz. = 100 C, 9 GC
Drambuie, 1 oz. = 110 C, 11 GC
Tia Maria, 1 oz. = 113 C, 9 GC
SPIRITS
Bourbon, brandy, Cognac, Canadian whiskey, gin, rye, rum, scotch, tequila and vodka are all carbohydrate free! The calories they contain depend upon the proof.
80 proof, 1 oz. = 67 C
84 proof, 1 oz. = 70 C
90 proof, 1 oz. = 75 C
94 proof, 1 oz. = 78 C
97 proof, 1 oz. = 81 C
100 proof, 1 oz. = 83 C

*C = calories
**GC = grams of carbohydrates

stocks, bouillons and consommes

When I started working on this book, one of the first things I had to decide was whether to change my basic stock recipes from those published in my first cookbook, *The Calculating Cook.* I had already spent two years perfecting the seasonings for my stocks in my first book. After several attempts at change—strictly for the sake of change—I decided it was ridiculous to alter recipes I had worked so hard to perfect, especially when basic stocks are so important to so many recipes for this book. Therefore, my stock recipes remain as they appeared in *The Calculating Cook.*

Again, may I emphasize the importance of making your own basic stocks. It is so easy once you get in the habit, and they make such a difference in flavor and are far less expensive than using bottled stock base, bouillon cubes or canned bouillon and consommés. There are a few exceptions to this rule: when your own basic stocks have either too much or incorrect seasoning for a special recipe. An example of this is found in my recipe for Cold Caviar Soup. The flavor of both my beef stock and chicken stock is too strong and detracts from the taste of the caviar. For this reason, I use canned beef consommé. But, this is a rare exception.

BEEF STOCK

3 pounds beef or veal bones	3 garlic buds	1 teaspoon salt
cold water to cover by 1 inch	2 parsley sprigs	defatted beef drippings (optional)
1 pound meat (optional)	2 whole cloves	cold water to cover by 1 inch
2 carrots, scraped and cut in pieces	1/4 teaspoon thyme	
2 stalks celery, without leaves	1/4 teaspoon marjoram	Makes about 2-1/2 quarts (10 cups)
1 onion, cut in half	1 bay leaf	Free food, calories negligible
1 tomato, cut in half	10 peppercorns	0 cholesterol when defatted

In a large pot or soup kettle, put the bones and enough cold water to cover by 1 inch. Bring them to a boil. Simmer slowly for 5 minutes and remove any scum that forms on the top. Add remaining ingredients and enough more cold water to cover by 1 inch. Cover, leaving the lid ajar about 1 inch to allow the steam to escape and simmer very slowly for at least 5 hours. Ten hours are even better, if you will be around to turn off the heat! When the stock has finished cooking, allow it to come to room temperature and put it in the refrigerator, uncovered, overnight. When the fat has hardened on the surface it can be easily removed. After removing every bit of fat, warm the stock until it becomes liquid. Strain the liquid and add more salt to taste, if needed.

If the flavor of your stock is too weak, you can boil it down to evaporate more of the liquid and concentrate its strength. (I always do this.) Store the stock in the freezer. I like to put some of it in 1-cup containers and some of it in ice-cube trays for individual servings. (Two cubes equals 1/4 cup.)

EASY METHOD: Dissolve 2 beef bouillon cubes or 2 teaspoons powdered beef stock base in 2 cups boiling water.

VARIATION: *Brown Stock* The ingredients for Brown Stock are the same as for Beef Stock. Preheat oven to 400°. Brown bones and meat for 30 minutes. Add carrots, celery and onions and brown together for another 30 minutes, or until a rich brown in color. Put the browned meat and vegetables in a large pot with the remaining ingredients, adding cold water to cover by 1 inch. Cover, leaving the lid ajar about 1 inch to allow the steam to escape, and simmer very slowly for at least 5 hours. Proceed exactly as you do for Beef Stock.

stocks, bouillons and consommes

CHICKEN STOCK

3 pounds chicken parts, wings,
   backs, etc.
1 whole stewing chicken (optional)
2 carrots, scraped and cut in pieces
2 stalks celery, without leaves

1 onion, cut in half
2 garlic buds
1 bay leaf
1/4 teaspoon basil
8 peppercorns

1 teaspoon salt
cold water to cover by 1 inch

Makes about 2-1/2 quarts (10 cups)
Free food, calories negligible
0 cholesterol when defatted

Put the chicken parts, whole chicken (if you are going to cook one), vegetables and spices in an 8- to 10-quart pot or soup kettle. Add cold water to cover by 1 inch. Bring slowly to a boil. Cover, leaving lid ajar about 1 inch to allow steam to escape. Simmer very slowly for 3 hours or until whole chicken is tender. Remove chicken and continue to simmer stock for 3 or 4 hours. Cool stock to room temperature and proceed exactly as you do for Beef Stock, page 23. Cooking the stewing chicken is helpful in two ways. First, it adds flavor to the stock. And second, it gives you a beautifully seasoned chicken for your dinner or many other dishes hot or cold.

EASY METHOD: Dissolve 2 chicken bouillon cubes or 2 teaspoons powdered chicken stock base in 2 cups boiling water.

TURKEY STOCK

1 turkey carcass
1 onion, cut in quarters
1 carrot, scraped and cut in pieces
2 bay leaves
1/2 teaspoon basil

1/4 teaspoon thyme
1/4 teaspoon marjoram
1 teaspoon salt
8 peppercorns
defatted turkey drippings (optional)
cold water to cover by 1 inch

Makes about 1-1/2 to 2 quarts (6 to
   8 cups)
Free food, calories negligible
0 cholesterol when defatted

Break up the turkey carcass and put it in a 8- to 10-quart pot or soup kettle. Add the vegetables and spices and cold water to cover by 1 inch. Cover, leaving the lid ajar about 1 inch to allow steam to escape. Simmer slowly for 4 hours. Cool to room temperature and proceed exactly as you do for Beef Stock, page 23.

FISH STOCK

2-1/2 quarts water
2 pounds fish heads, bones and
    trimmings
2 onions, sliced
5 parsley sprigs

1 carrot, sliced
1/2 teaspoon marjoram
4 peppercorns
1 teaspoon salt
1 tablespoon freshly squeezed
    lemon juice

Makes 2 quarts (8 cups)
Free food, calories negligible
0 cholesterol when defatted

Bring all of the ingredients to a boil and simmer for 40 minutes. Line a colander or strainer with damp cheesecloth and strain the fish stock through it. Cool and keep refrigerated. If you are not planning to use the fish stock for 2 days or more, put it in the freezer.

COURT BOUILLON

4 cups water
1/4 cup white vinegar
1/2 lemon, sliced
1 celery stalk, sliced
1 carrot, sliced

1/2 onion, sliced
1 garlic bud
1 bay leaf
6 peppercorns
1-1/2 teaspoons salt

Makes 1 quart (4 cups)
Free food, calories negligible
0 cholesterol

Anytime you are going to cook shrimp, crab or lobster, or poach any fish, prepare a court bouillon first. Of course you can use fish stock for poaching fish, but this court bouillon is much faster and easier to make and completely satisfactory. You just cannot compare seafood cooked in plain, salty water to the seafood cooked in court bouillon. Always be careful not to overcook seafood because overcooking makes it tough. For example, when cooking shrimp never allow them to boil more than 2 minutes. Then cool them in the court bouillon.

Combine all of the above ingredients and cook for 45 minutes. This court bouillon may be made ahead and used many times. When doing this, strain before storing. After each use, store in the freezer.

stocks, bouillons and consommes

CHICKEN AND BEEF BOUILLON

1 part Chicken Stock, page 24 or Beef Stock, page 23	1 part water	Free food, calories negligible 0 cholesterol when defatted

Put the stock and water in a pan and bring to a boil. Simmer for at least 15 minutes before using. Basically, bouillons are just weak stocks. For this reason I find it troublesome and confusing to actually make both stocks and bouillons from scratch. Troublesome, because I think the bouillon made from a good, rich stock has a better flavor than most other bouillons, and confusing because I have enough trouble keeping track of everything in my freezer as it is. Bouillon is fabulous for cooking vegetables, as it adds so much flavor and no food value.

BEEF CONSOMMÉ
(Clarified Beef Stock)

2 egg whites	1 parsley sprig	Makes 1 quart (4 cups)
4 cups Beef Stock, page 23	2 green onion tops, chopped	Free food, calories negligible
3 tablespoons lean ground beef	1 carrot, chopped	0 cholesterol when defatted
1/2 teaspoon chervil	salt to taste	

If you are going to serve consommé hot or cold, you will want it beautifully clear. The addition of egg whites clarifies it. Beat the egg whites with a wire whisk until they are slightly foamy. Add 1 cup of the cold stock to the egg whites and beat lightly together. Put the other 3 cups of stock in a very clean saucepan with all remaining ingredients. (It is not necessary to add the other ingredients, but the consommé will have a much better flavor if you do!) Bring the stock to a boil and remove from the heat. Slowly pour the egg white and stock mixture into the stock, stirring with the wire whisk as you do. Put the saucepan back on a very low heat and mix gently until it starts to simmer. Put the pan half on the heat and half off so that it is barely simmering, turning the pan around every few minutes. Simmer for 40 minutes. Line a colander or a strainer with 2 or 3 layers of damp cheesecloth. Allow it to drain, undisturbed, until it has all seeped through. Then store until ready to use.

VARIATIONS: If you are serving the consommé hot, just before serving add 2 tablespoons Madeira. If you are planning to serve the consommé cold and want it firm, or if you are going to use it for aspics or molded salads, add 2 tablespoons Sherry and 1 envelope unflavored gelatin dissolved in 1/4 cup cold water to every 2 cups of consommé while still hot.

CHICKEN CONSOMMÉ

4 cups Chicken Stock, page 24,
  with all fat removed
2 egg whites
1 bay leaf

1 parsley sprig
2 green onion tops, chopped
1 carrot, chopped
salt to taste

Makes 1 quart (4 cups)
Free food, calories negligible
0 cholesterol when defatted

Proceed exactly as you do for Beef Consommé, preceding.

CONSOMMÉ MADRILENE

3 large, ripe tomatoes, sliced
2 stalks celery, chopped
1 leek, white part only, chopped
1 carrot, sliced
1 onion, sliced
1 teaspoon freshly squeezed lemon
  juice

6 peppercorns
2 quarts Chicken Stock, page 24
2 bay leaves
2 envelopes unflavored gelatin
1/4 cup cold water

2 drops red food coloring (optional)
salt and freshly ground black pepper
  to taste

Makes 1 to 1-1/2 quarts (4 to 6 cups)
Free food, calories negligible
0 cholesterol when defatted

Place vegetables, lemon juice, peppercorns, stock and bay leaves in a large pot or soup kettle. Cover, leaving the lid ajar about 1 inch to allow steam to escape. Simmer for 2 hours. Soften gelatin in 1/4 cup water. Add the 2 drops of red food coloring, if desired, for better color. Add gelatin mixture to hot consommé and stir until completely dissolved. Cool slightly and strain through a fine strainer. Season to taste with salt and pepper. Cool to room temperature and refrigerate. When consommé is completely jelled, unmold and cut off the part containing the sediment. Cut up the clear part and serve in sherbet glasses or cups.

soups hot and cold

Soups, both hot and cold, are more fun when they are a bit unusual. Surprise your friends by starting your next dinner party with a deliciously different cold soup served in an icer. Your guests will all think by looking at it that it is a calorie-packed vichyssoise *until* they taste your Potage of Celery Root. Even your children will rave over your Cream of Fresh Tomato Soup. When you can't spare an extra calorie or milligram of cholesterol in the soup course, serve Egg Sprout Soup with a dash of soy sauce!

COLD CRANBERRY SOUP

1 cup water
1 cinnamon stick, broken in half
3 tablespoons quick-cooking tapioca
1 teaspoon finely grated lemon peel

2-1/2 cups artificially sweetened
    cranberry juice
2-1/2 cups unsweetened pineapple
    juice
1/4 cup Port wine

Makes 8 servings
Each serving contains:
approximately 1 fruit portion
40 calories
0 cholesterol

Bring water and cinnamon stick to a boil. Add tapioca and cook, stirring occasionally, for 5 minutes. Remove from heat and add grated lemon peel. Cool to room temperature. Add cranberry juice, pineapple juice and Port. Refrigerate, if possible, 24 hours before serving. Serve in icers. This is a good appetizer for the holidays.

soups hot and cold

COLD CAVIAR SOUP

2 cups canned, beef consommé
1 cup low-fat Jelled Milk, page 39
1/2 cup sour cream or imitation
   sour cream
1 tablespoon freshly squeezed
   lemon juice
4 ounces caviar (the best your budget
   will allow!)

1/2 cup minced onion
2 hard-boiled eggs, whites
   only, shredded
parsley sprigs for garnish

Makes 8 servings

Each serving contains:
1/2 fat portion
1/2 protein portion
60 calories
97.65 milligrams cholesterol with
   sour cream
42.75 milligrams cholesterol with
   imitation sour cream

Put all ingredients, except caviar, eggs and onion, into blender and blend until thoroughly mixed. Pour the mixture into a large bowl. Add the caviar and onions and mix thoroughly with a wire whisk. Chill well before serving. Serve this soup in icers. Sprinkle each serving with shredded hard-boiled egg whites. Garnish each serving with sprig of parsley for color.

CHILLED POTAGE OF CELERY ROOT

2 small celery roots
   (or 1 very large one)
1-1/2 cups buttermilk
3/4 teaspoon salt

dash of white pepper
2 drops yellow food coloring
1/2 cup finely chopped chives
   or green onion tops

Makes 6 servings

Each serving contains:
1 B vegetable portion
1/4 milk portion
56 calories
3.8 milligrams cholesterol

Peel the celery root and dice into 1/2-inch cubes. Place celery root in steamer and steam over boiling water for 10 minutes, or until tender enough to be easily mashed. Remove celery root from steamer and reserve 1 cup of the liquid. Put one-third of the celery root and the reserved cooking liquid in a blender. Blend until smooth, alternately adding the remaining celery root and buttermilk, salt, white pepper and food coloring. Blend until velvety smooth. Pour into a mixing bowl and mix thoroughly with the chopped chives. Chill before serving. If possible, serve in icers.

FRESH MUSHROOM BISQUE

2 tablespoons corn oil
1/4 cup minced celery
1/4 cup minced onion
2-1/2 tablespoons flour
1 cup chicken stock, boiling
1-1/2 cups low-fat milk, warmed
1/2 teaspoon salt
1/8 teaspoon ground nutmeg

1/8 teaspoon white pepper
1/8 teaspoon tarragon
4 teaspoons corn oil margarine
2 cups thinly sliced fresh mushrooms
2 tablespoons Sherry
1/2 cup minced parsley
2 tablespoons Toasted Almond Flakes
   (14 almonds), page 45

Makes 6 servings
Each serving contains:
2 fat portions
1/4 milk portion
120 calories
3.9 milligrams cholesterol

Heat corn oil in a large saucepan. Add celery and onions and cook until onion is clear and slightly soft. Add flour and cook, stirring constantly, for 3 minutes, being careful not to brown the flour. Add the boiling chicken stock *all at once,* rapidly stirring with a wire whisk. Cook until thickened. Slowly add the warm milk, salt, nutmeg, white pepper and tarragon. Continue cooking over low heat while you cook the mushrooms.

In a cured heavy iron skillet, melt the corn oil margarine. Add the sliced mushrooms and cook until tender. Add the mushrooms to the soup mixture. Just before serving, add the Sherry. Sprinkle the top of each bowl with parsley and Toasted Almond Flakes.

soups hot and cold

CREAM OF FRESH TOMATO SOUP

6 large ripe tomatoes
1 tablespoon corn oil margarine
1-1/2 tablespoons minced onion
2 teaspoons arrowroot
1 cup water

3 cups low-fat milk
1-1/4 teaspoons salt
dash of white pepper
1 more tablespoon corn oil margarine

Makes 6 servings

Each serving contains:
1/2 milk portion
1 fat portion
85 calories
7.75 milligrams cholesterol

Peel and seed the tomatoes. This is most easily done by dipping them in boiling water for several seconds, which loosens the skin and makes it simple to remove. Cut the tomatoes in half crosswise and squeeze the seeds from them, carefully removing any remaining seeds with a grapefruit spoon. Chop the tomatoes into small pieces. Melt margarine in a large saucepan and add the onion. Cook until the onion is soft and clear. Add the tomatoes and cook, covered, over medium heat, stirring occasionally, until the tomatoes are very soft. This takes about 30 minutes.

While the tomatoes are cooking, dissolve the arrowroot in 1/2 cup of cold water. Add the remaining 1/2 cup of water and in a saucepan bring mixture to a slow boil over medium heat, stirring constantly until thickened; set aside. Put the cooked tomatoes and onion in a blender with 1 cup of milk and blend until a smooth, creamy consistency. Pour back into the large saucepan and add the arrowroot mixture and remaining 2 cups of milk, salt and white pepper, mixing thoroughly with a wire whisk. Put the saucepan back on medium heat and bring to serving temperature. *Do not boil.* Just before serving, add the remaining tablespoon of margarine and mix thoroughly.

EGG SPROUT SOUP
(This is before it flowers!)

3 cups chicken stock
2 egg whites
1 cup bean sprouts

1 tablespoon soy sauce
2 tablespoons finely chopped chives
    or green onion tops

Makes 4 servings
Free food, calories negligible
0 cholesterol

Bring the chicken stock to a boil. Beat the egg whites with a fork until slightly frothy. Steam the bean sprouts until tender crisp, about 2 or 3 minutes. Slowly pour the beaten egg whites into the boiling chicken stock, stirring constantly with a wire whisk. Add the bean sprouts and soy sauce. Serve very hot. Sprinkle the top of each bowl with the chopped chives or green onion tops. Put soy sauce on the table for those who wish additional soy sauce in their soup.

RUSSIAN BORSCHT

2 cups shredded beets
1/2 cup shredded carrots
1/2 cup shredded onion
1 cup water
3 cups beef stock

2 cups shredded cabbage
1 tablespoon freshly squeezed
    lemon juice
6 tablespoons sour cream

Makes 6 servings

Each serving contains:
1 group B vegetable portion
1/2 fat portion
41 calories
8 milligrams cholesterol

Put beets, carrots and onion in a large soup kettle. Add the water and 2 cups of the beef stock. Cook over medium heat until all vegetables are tender, about 20 minutes. Add the shredded cabbage and remaining 1 cup of beef stock and cook for 15 minutes. Add the lemon juice. Serve hot with 1 tablespoon sour cream on top of each serving.

sauces and gravies

God bless the French! What would we do without their sauces? *And,* God help *me* when the French read my recipes for some of their classics! My Brown, Béarnaise and French Herb Sauces are a giant step away from their classic French cousins in ingredients, *but* only inches away in taste. When you consider the vast difference in calories, cholesterol and saturated fats between my recipes and the original versions, I think you will agree with me that a little less richness can be easily tolerated. I believe you will also find after you have been making your own "French sauces" for a while that the more classic versions will seem much too rich to you. At least, I hope so!

DEFATTED DRIPPINGS

Free food, calories negligible
0 cholesterol when defatted

If you love gravy but don't eat it because it's *fat, fat, fat,* then one of your problems is solved. Just defat your drippings!

All drippings are defatted in the same manner. After cooking your roast beef, leg of lamb, chicken, turkey or whatever, remove it from the roasting pan and pour the drippings into a bowl. Put the bowl in the refrigerator until the drippings are cold and all of the fat has solidified on the top. Remove the fat and you have defatted drippings!

Now, if you are in a hurry for them because you want to serve your roast beef au jus with defatted drippings instead of "fat jus," then put the drippings in the freezer instead of the refrigerator. Put the roast in a warm oven to keep it from getting cold. After about 20 minutes you can remove the fat, heat the jus and serve.

I always defat my drippings when I roast meat or poultry and keep them in the freezer. Defatted drippings add extra flavor to your stocks and are better than stocks for making the Skinny Gravies.

sauces and gravies

SKINNY BEEF GRAVY

1 cup Defatted Beef Drippings,
   page 35
1 cup beef stock

2 tablespoons cornstarch or arrowroot
1/4 cup water
salt to taste

Makes 1 to 1-1/2 cups
Free food, calories negligible
0 cholesterol

Heat the Defatted Beef Drippings and beef stock in a saucepan. Mix the water with cornstarch or arrowroot and add to the gravy. Cook over medium heat, stirring occasionally, until thickened. Add salt to taste. Beef stock can be stored in ice cube trays in the freezer and used for individual servings of this gravy. For 1 serving, use: 2 beef stock cubes, 1/4 teaspoon cornstarch or arrowroot and 1 teaspoon chopped onion (optional).

SKINNY TURKEY MUSHROOM GRAVY

2 cups Defatted Turkey Drippings,
   page 35
2 cups beef stock
3 tablespoons cornstarch or arrowroot

1/4 cup water
2 teaspoons corn oil margarine
1/2 cup sliced fresh mushrooms
salt and freshly ground black pepper

Makes 2 to 3 cups
Free food, calories negligible
0 cholesterol

Heat the Defatted Turkey Drippings and beef stock in a saucepan. Dissolve the cornstarch or arrowroot in water and add to gravy. Cook slowly over medium heat, stirring occasionally, until mixture thickens slightly. While the gravy is cooking, heat the margarine in a skillet and add the sliced mushrooms. Cook until tender and add to the gravy. Season to taste with salt and pepper.

BROWN SAUCE

1 quart Beef Stock, page 23
1 tablespoon finely chopped shallots
1/2 cup Burgundy
1/4 cup Sherry
1/4 cup dry white wine (I prefer
 Chablis)

4 tablespoons cornstarch
1/4 cup cold water
1/2 teaspoon salt
dash of freshly ground black pepper
2 teaspoons Kitchen Bouquet
3 drops red food coloring

Makes 4 scant cups
Each 1/2 cup contains:
1/4 starch portion
17 calories
0 cholesterol

In a saucepan, heat the Beef Stock. In another pan combine the chopped shallots and wines and heat over fairly high heat, boiling it until it has reduced by one-third in volume. When reduced, add the heated Beef Stock to the wine and then lower the heat to medium. Allow the mixture to come again to a simmering boil. Mix the cornstarch and water until completely dissolved. Add the cornstarch mixture to the sauce, mixing thoroughly using a wire whisk. Season to taste with salt and pepper. To get the rich dark brown color associated with the classic French brown sauce, add the Kitchen Bouquet and red food coloring.

Brown Sauce is a necessary ingredient for such classics as coq au vin, osso buco and cassoulet. It can also make a simple broiled ground-round patty an epicurean delight.

BROWN ONIONS

2-1/2 pounds onions (4 large onions)
1 teaspoon corn oil

Makes approximately 2 cups

Each 1/2 cup contains:
1 B vegetable portion
36 calories
0 cholesterol

The number of onions depends upon the amount of glazed onions desired. I use at least 4 large onions because if I am not using all of them, I can put the remainder in the refrigerator and reheat to use as a garnish on steaks, chops, meat patties, or, even chicken!

Peel and slice onions very thinly. Pour the corn oil into a cured heavy iron skillet. Using a paper towel, wipe corn oil over entire inner surface of the skillet. Heat the skillet over medium heat and add the thinly sliced onions. Cook over medium heat, stirring frequently, for 30 minutes. Continue cooking onions, stirring occasionally, over low heat for another 30 minutes, or a little longer if necessary to lightly brown the onions.

sauces and gravies

BASIC WHITE SAUCE

2 cups low-fat milk
1 tablespoon corn oil margarine
2-1/2 tablespoons sifted flour
1/8 teaspoon salt

Makes 1-1/2 cups

Each recipe (1-1/2 cups) contains:
3 fat portions
1 starch portion
2 milk portions
453 calories
31 milligrams cholesterol

Each 1/2 recipe (3/4 cup) contains:
1-1/2 fat portions
1/2 starch portion
1 milk portion
226 calories
15.5 milligrams cholesterol

Put the milk in a saucepan on low heat and bring to boiling point. In another saucepan melt the margarine and add the flour, stirring constantly. Cook the flour and margarine for 3 minutes. *Do not brown.* Take the flour-margarine mixture off of the heat and add the simmering milk all at once, stirring constantly with a wire whisk. Put the sauce back on low heat and cook slowly for 30 minutes, stirring occasionally. (If you wish a thicker sauce, cook it a little longer.) Add the salt. If there are lumps in the sauce (though there shouldn't be by this method), put it in the blender!

MILK GLAZE

1 cup fish or chicken stock
2 cups low-fat milk
2 envelopes unflavored gelatin

1/2 cup cold water
1/2 teaspoon salt

Free food, calories negligible
Entire recipe contains:
31 milligrams cholesterol

Heat the stock and milk together. Soften the gelatin in the cold water. Add the gelatin to the milk and stock. Add the salt and stir until the gelatin is dissolved completely. *Do not boil.* Cool slightly and pour over cold poultry or fish to glaze and decorate.

This recipe may easily be cut in half for smaller portions. It is fun to glaze and decorate a whole, cold chicken or turkey for a buffet. Decorate it with fresh fruit or vegetables cut in fancy shapes. I also love cold poached salmon done this way. The amount of milk in each portion is so small that this glaze does not really need to be counted on the diet program.

JELLED MILK

1/4 cup water
1 envelope unflavored gelatin
1 cup milk (non-fat, low-fat or
    buttermilk)

Makes 1 cup

Each cup contains:
1 milk portion
80 calories (non-fat or buttermilk)
125 calories (low-fat milk)

2.3 milligrams cholesterol with
    non-fat milk
15.5 milligrams cholesterol with
    low-fat milk
7.8 milligrams cholesterol with
    buttermilk

Put the water in a small saucepan. Sprinkle the gelatin on the top and allow it to soften for 5 minutes. Place the saucepan on low heat, stirring constantly, until the gelatin is completely dissolved. *Do not allow it to come to a boil.* Slowly pour the milk into the gelatin, stirring as you do. Place the gelatin-milk mixture in the refrigerator. When it is jelled, it is ready to use as Jelled Milk for many recipes.

I think it is a good idea to keep some Jelled Milk in the refrigerator to use at any time in such recipes as Cold Caviar Soup, Green Goodness Dressing, Prune Mousse, et cetera. I prefer equal portions of plain cold milk and Jelled Milk mixed in the blender, poured over fruit or breakfast cereal, to just plain milk. It makes the dish seem so much richer.

sauces and gravies

FRENCH HERB SAUCE

1 tablespoon tarragon
1 tablespoon chervil
1 bay leaf
1/8 teaspoon salt
dash of white pepper
dash of thyme
1/2 cup white wine vinegar
2 tablespoons tomato purée
2 tablespoons finely chopped shallots

2 tablespoons arrowroot
1 cup water
1 cup Basic White Sauce, page 38
1/4 teaspoon freshly squeezed
    lemon juice
dash of paprika

Makes 2 scant cups

Each recipe contains:
2 fat portions
1 starch portion
1 milk portion
283 calories
15.5 milligrams cholesterol
2 tablespoons contain:
1/4 fat portion
18 calories
1 milligram cholesterol

Crush tarragon, chervil and bay leaf using a mortar and pestle. Combine in saucepan with other herbs and spices, vinegar, tomato purée and shallots, and over medium heat reduce to one-third of original volume. Allow the mixture to cool to room temperature.

Mix the arrowroot with the cold water until completely dissolved. Heat over medium heat until it comes to a boil and becomes clear and thickened. Remove from heat and allow to cool.

When both arrowroot mixture and herb-sauce mixture have cooled to room temperature, pour them into a large mixing bowl and mix together thoroughly using a wire whisk. Add the white sauce to this mixture and using a wire whisk again, mix thoroughly. Pour the sauce through a sieve and carefully press all of the sauce through the sieve using the back of a wooden spoon so that only the solid particles remain in the sieve.

Just before using the sauce, add the lemon juice and mix carefully. I like this sauce on fish. However it is also good served over many other dishes. Sprinkle with paprika sparingly before serving.

sauces and gravies

SIMPLE HOLLANDAISE SAUCE

1/2 cup cold water
1 tablespoon arrowroot
3/4 cup safflower oil mayonnaise
4 tablespoons corn oil margarine

2 teaspoons freshly squeezed
  lemon juice

Makes 1-1/2 cups

1 tablespoon contains:
2 fat portions
90 calories
4 milligrams cholesterol

Mix the arrowroot with cold water until completely dissolved. Heat over medium heat until mixture comes to a boil, stirring constantly until it is clear and thickened. Remove from heat.

Put mayonnaise in an ovenproof casserole. Add the margarine and lemon juice. Place in a 300° oven for 5 minutes, or until margarine melts. Remove from oven and beat with wire whisk. Add arrowroot mixture and continue beating with wire whisk until smooth.

SIMPLE BÉARNAISE SAUCE

1-1/2 cups Simple Hollandaise Sauce,
  preceding
1 teaspoon finely minced fresh
  tarragon, or
1/2 teaspoon dry tarragon, or

1-1/2 teaspoons tarragon vinegar
1/2 teaspoon minced shallots
1/2 teaspoon finely minced parsley

Makes 1-1/2 cups (24 tablespoons)

1 tablespoon contains:
2 fat portions
90 calories
4 milligrams cholesterol

Combine all ingredients and mix well.

COOKED MUSTARD SAUCE

1/2 cup cider vinegar
1-1/2 tablespoons dry mustard
liquid egg substitute = 2 eggs
1/2 cup low-fat milk

1 tablespoon corn oil margarine
sugar substitute = 2 tablespoons sugar

Makes 1-1/2 cups

2 tablespoons contain:
1/4 fat portion
23 calories
.6 milligram cholesterol

Combine the mustard with the vinegar and stir until mustard has dissolved completely. Combine vinegar-mustard mixture with the liquid egg substitute and milk in a saucepan. Slowly bring to a boil, stirring constantly with wire whisk. Continue stirring and allow to simmer for *no more* than 1 minute. Remove from the heat and put the margarine on the top of the sauce. *Do not stir.* Allow to cool to room temperature. Add the sugar substitute and again, using a wire whisk, mix the margarine and sugar substitute thoroughly into the sauce. Store in the refrigerator.

This is an excellent sauce for cold meats and for Scandinavian Pickled Salmon.

MINT SAUCE

2 cups firmly packed chopped
   fresh mint leaves and stems
2-1/2 cups water
2 tablespoons arrowroot

2 tablespoons water
2 tablespoons freshly squeezed
   lemon juice
sugar substitute = 1/3 cup sugar
2 drops green food coloring

Makes about 2 cups
Free food, calories negligible
0 cholesterol

Put mint and water in a saucepan and bring to a boil. Remove from heat and allow to stand for 15 minutes. Strain and return liquid to saucepan. Mix arrowroot with water until thoroughly dissolved. Add to mint juice and bring to a boil. Simmer until slightly thickened. Remove from heat and allow to cool to room temperature. Add lemon juice, sugar substitute and green food coloring. Store in refrigerator.

sauces and gravies

SAUCE DILLY DILLY

1/2 cup safflower oil mayonnaise
1 cup low-fat plain yogurt
1/2 teaspoon salt

3/4 teaspoon tarragon
1-1/2 teaspoons dill weed

Makes 1-1/2 cups

1 tablespoon contains:
1 fat portion
approximately 45 calories
approximately 3 milligrams cholesterol

Put the safflower mayonnaise, low-fat yogurt and salt in a mixing bowl and mix thoroughly using a wire whisk. Crush the tarragon and dill weed thoroughly, using a mortar and pestle. Add the crushed mixture to the other ingredients and mix thoroughly. Pour into a container with a tight-fitting lid and refrigerate at least 2 days before using.

This sauce is used with recipes in this book, such as Dillied Fish Amandine and is also delicious used as a cold sauce for fish or vegetable dips.

TOMATO CHEESE TOPPING

1 tablespoon corn oil margarine
2 tablespoons minced onion
4 large fresh tomatoes, peeled and
   diced
1/2 teaspoon oregano

1/4 teaspoon salt
3/4 cup grated Cheddar cheese

Makes 6 servings

Each serving contains:
1/2 fat portion
1/2 protein portion
63 calories
15 milligrams cholesterol

Heat margarine in a cured heavy iron skillet. Add the onion and tomatoes and cook until onion is clear and tender. Using mortar and pestle, crush oregano and add to sauce. Add salt and mix thoroughly. Add Cheddar cheese and simmer slowly until cheese has melted.

This is a colorful as well as a delicious low-calorie sauce to serve with vegetables or meat.

CRANBERRY CHUTNEY

1 16-ounce can peeled tomatoes, including liquid
4 cups (1 pound) fresh cranberries
1 cup seedless raisins
1 teaspoon salt
sugar substitute = 1 cup sugar

1 teaspoon peeled and grated ginger root, or
1/2 teaspoon ground ginger

Makes approximately 5 cups

Each 1/2 cup contains:
1-1/2 fruit portions
60 calories
0 cholesterol
Each 1/4 cup contains:
3/4 fruit portion
30 calories
0 cholesterol

Cut up tomatoes in fairly large chunks. Combine tomatoes and juice from the can with all other ingredients in a large saucepan. Cover and bring to a slow boil over medium heat; simmer 15 minutes. Cool to room temperature and refrigerate in a tightly covered container for at least 2 days before serving. This is an excellent variation of the traditional cranberry sauce served with holiday meals. It is also excellent served with cold ham or roast beef.

TOASTED ALMOND FLAKES

shelled almonds (the quantity depends on the amount of almond flakes you want to make!)
salt

7 almonds = 1 fat portion or 45 calories
7 almonds makes 3 teaspoons Toasted Almond Flakes

42 almonds = 1/2 cup
0 cholesterol

Place number of almonds desired on a cutting board and mince with a sharp knife, as you would parsley or chives. *Do not* put them in the blender because often you will be using so few almonds you will turn them into a paste rather than getting the desired flaky texture. Place the almond flakes on a cookie sheet and lightly salt them. Place under the broiler, watching constantly because they burn quickly. Toast them to the desired brownness. (I like mine very toasted.)

The advantage of using Toasted Almond Flakes in recipes instead of sliced or chopped almonds is that they are light in texture and can be sprinkled like snowflakes onto salads, entrées or desserts. It also requires far fewer almonds to get the same amount of flavor, thereby cutting the fat portion and calories down tremendously. Toasted Almond Flakes should not be prepared ahead and stored, because they will lose a great deal of their flavor.

salad dressings

For anyone who likes salads as much as I do, the Salad Dressings section is a very important part of a cookbook.

Therefore, I am giving it a heading all its own in this book. In this chapter, I try to offer you a wide variety of choices, both in flavor range and calorie content. It is important to have dressings which are practically calorie-free to balance a daily menu already containing all of your *allowed* fats in other foods. However, occasionally it is fun to save up the fats allowed for the whole day and put them *all* on one gorgeous salad!

GARLIC-FLAVORED OIL

1 cup corn oil	Makes 1 cup	1 fat portion
2 garlic buds, peeled and quartered	1 teaspoon contains:	45 calories
		0 cholesterol

Place the corn oil and the garlic in a jar with a tight-fitting lid and allow to stand at room temperature for a full 24 hours. Remove garlic from the oil. Store in the refrigerator for various uses, such as, croutons for Caesar salad, garlic-flavored oil for salad dressing, sautéing onions, et cetera.

salad dressings

HAPPY HEART DRESSING

1 tablespoon salt
1/2 cup red wine vinegar
sugar substitute = 1/2 teaspoon sugar
1/2 teaspoon freshly ground black
   pepper

1 tablespoon freshly squeezed lemon
   juice
1-1/2 teaspoons Worcestershire sauce
1/2 teaspoon Dijon-style mustard
1/2 garlic bud, minced
1/2 cup water
2 cups corn oil

Makes 3 cups
1 tablespoon contains:
2 fat portions
90 calories
0 cholesterol

Dissolve salt in the vinegar. Add all other ingredients except oil and mix well. Slowly stir in the oil. Place in a jar with a tight-fitting lid and shake vigorously for a full minute. Store in refrigerator. This is a larger quantity of dressing than I usually give for recipes in my book, but this keeps well and is the basis for several other dressings.

HAPPY HEART TARRAGON DRESSING

1 cup Happy Heart Dressing, preceding
1 teaspoon tarragon

Makes 1 cup
1 tablespoon contains:
2 fat portions

90 calories
0 cholesterol

Using a mortar and pestle, crush the tarragon completely. Add to the Happy Heart Dressing and mix thoroughly.

HAPPY HEART VINAIGRETTE DRESSING

1 cup Happy Heart Dressing, page 48
1 tablespoon capers, finely chopped
1 tablespoon pimiento, finely chopped
1 teaspoon finely chopped chives

1 teaspoon finely chopped parsley
1 hard-boiled egg white, finely chopped
1/8 teaspoon paprika

Makes approximately 1-1/4 cups

1 tablespoon contains:
approximately 2 fat portions
90 calories
0 cholesterol

Add all ingredients to Happy Heart Dressing and mix thoroughly. I approach vinaigrette dressing much the way the French housewife approaches a cassoulet—I chop up whatever is handy and put it in! For example, sometimes I add minced celery or some cold cooked vegetable, finely minced. Pickles are sometimes also a nice addition. It depends on what you are using the dressing for.

HAPPY HEART CURRY DRESSING

1 cup Happy Heart Dressing, page 48
1/4 teaspoon curry powder
1/8 teaspoon ground ginger

Makes 1 cup
1 tablespoon contains:

2 fat portions
90 calories
0 cholesterol

Add the curry powder and ginger to the Happy Heart Dressing and mix thoroughly. This amount of curry creates a very subtle flavor. In fact, so subtle that you will find many guests will ask you what the seasoning is in your dressing. If you wish a stronger curry flavor, increase the curry powder to 1/2 teaspoon. For a *very* strong curry flavor increase to 1 full teaspoon of curry powder. Personally, I like it best when it is very subtle and mysterious!

salad dressings

HAPPY HEART CUMIN DRESSING

1 cup Happy Heart Dressing, page 48
1/4 teaspoon ground cumin

Makes 1 cup
1 tablespoon contains:

2 fat portions
90 calories
0 cholesterol

Add cumin to Happy Heart Dressing and mix thoroughly. The flavor of this dressing is better if allowed to stand for 24 hours before using. If you prefer a stronger cumin flavor, add a little more cumin to the dressing.

HAPPY HEART GARLIC DRESSING

3 garlic buds, peeled and quartered
2 cups corn oil
1 tablespoon salt
1/2 cup red wine vinegar
sugar substitute = 1/2 teaspoon sugar
1/2 cup water

1/2 teaspoon freshly ground black
    pepper
1 tablespoon freshly squeezed lemon
    juice
1-1/2 teaspoons Worcestershire sauce
1/2 teaspoon Dijon-style mustard
1/2 garlic bud, minced

Makes 3 cups
1 tablespoon contains:
2 fat portions
90 calories
0 cholesterol

Twenty-four hours before making this dressing, add the 3 garlic buds to the corn oil and put it in a jar with tight-fitting lid. Allow to stand at room temperature for a full 24 hours. Remove the garlic from the oil. Dissolve the salt in the vinegar. Add all ingredients except garlic oil and mix well. Slowly stir in the oil. Place in a jar with a tight-fitting lid and shake vigorously for a full minute. Store in the refrigerator. This dressing is good as it is—if you like garlic! It is also the basic dressing for my Happy Heart Caesar Dressing.

HAPPY HEART ITALIAN DRESSING

1 cup Happy Heart Dressing, page 48
1 teaspoon oregano
1/2 teaspoon sweet basil
1/2 teaspoon tarragon

sugar substitute = 1/4 teaspoon

Makes 1 cup
1 tablespoon contains:

2 fat portions
90 calories
0 cholesterol

Add all ingredients to Happy Heart Dressing and mix thoroughly. This dressing makes an excellent marinade for cold cooked vegetables to be served as an antipasto—the first course of an Italian meal.

salad dressings

HAPPY HEART CAESAR DRESSING

3 cups Happy Heart Garlic Dressing,
  page 50
1/4 cup freshly squeezed lemon juice
1/2 cup grated Parmesan cheese
1 2-ounce can drained anchovy fillets,
  finely chopped

Makes 3 cups
1 tablespoon contains:
approximately 2 fat portions
90 calories
.6 milligram cholesterol

The protein content for the anchovies
in 1 tablespoon of dressing is so slight
that it need not be calculated.

Add all ingredients to Happy Heart Garlic Dressing and mix thoroughly. This Caesar salad dressing is *so* good that several Caesar salad buffs who had this in my home stated it was the best Caesar Salad they had ever eaten! I made no comment. Wouldn't they have been surprised if they had known that an egg never came close to their salad.

MYSTERY SALAD DRESSING

1/2 cup Jelled Buttermilk, page 39
1/2 cup cold buttermilk
2 teaspoons garlic salt
sugar substitute = 1/2 teaspoon sugar
6 tablespoons soy sauce

2 tablespoons freshly squeezed lemon
  juice
2 tablespoons corn oil
1 tablespoon Worcestershire sauce
2 teaspoons white vinegar
1 teaspoon prepared brown mustard

Makes 1-1/2 cups
1 tablespoon contains:
1/4 fat portion
12 calories
.7 milligram cholesterol

Put all ingredients in blender. Blend until smooth.

WHITE WINE SALAD DRESSING

1/2 cup tarragon vinegar
1 teaspoon dry mustard
1 teaspoon salt
sugar substitute = 1 teaspoon sugar
1 teaspoon tarragon

1 teaspoon sweet basil
1/4 teaspoon celery seed
1/2 teaspoon Worcestershire sauce
1/4 cup dry white wine (I use Chablis)
3/4 cup corn oil

Makes 1-1/2 cups
1 tablespoon contains:
1-1/2 fat portions
68 calories
0 cholesterol

Pour the vinegar into a jar with a tight-fitting lid. Add dry mustard, salt and sugar substitute. Mix thoroughly until salt and mustard are completely dissolved. Using a mortar and pestle, crush the tarragon, sweet basil and celery seed together. Add to the vinegar mixture, mixing thoroughly again. Add the Worcestershire sauce and wine; mix. Add the corn oil and shake for 30 seconds. Store in refrigerator. You will find this dressing improves in flavor if allowed to stand 1 or 2 days before using.

RED WINE VINEGAR DRESSING

1/3 cup red wine vinegar
1 teaspoon salt
sugar substitute = 1/2 teaspoon sugar
1/2 teaspoon dry mustard
1/8 teaspoon freshly ground black
   pepper

1/2 teaspoon sweet basil
1/2 teaspoon tarragon
1/2 teaspoon oregano
1/2 teaspoon Worcestershire sauce
1 tablespoon red wine
1/2 cup corn oil

Makes approximately 1 cup
1 tablespoon contains:
1-1/2 fat portions
68 calories
0 cholesterol

Combine the red wine vinegar with the salt, sugar substitute and dry mustard and mix until the salt and mustard are completely dissolved in the vinegar. Add the pepper. Crush basil, tarragon and oregano together using a mortar and pestle. Add to vinegar mixture and again mix thoroughly. Add the red wine. Slowly stir in the oil and place in a jar with a tight-fitting lid. Shake vigorously for 30 seconds. Chill before serving.

salad dressings

TROPICAL SALAD DRESSING

1/2 cup unsweetened pineapple juice
1 tablespoon soy sauce
1 tablespoon Champagne vinegar
sugar substitute = 1/2 teaspoon sugar

1/4 teaspoon coconut extract
1/2 cup corn oil

Makes 1-1/4 cups

1 tablespoon contains:
1-1/4 fat portions
56 calories
0 cholesterol

Combine all ingredients except corn oil and shake well. Slowly stir in the corn oil and shake for 30 seconds. Refrigerate before using. This makes a lovely dressing for fruit salad. It is also very good on cold chicken or fish.

DIJON MUSTARD DRESSING

1 teaspoon arrowroot
1/4 cup water
3 tablespoons white wine vinegar
1/4 teaspoon salt

1/8 teaspoon white pepper
2 tablespoons Dijon-style mustard
1/2 cup corn oil
1/2 cup low-fat milk

Makes 1-1/3 cups
1 tablespoon contains:
1 fat portion
54 calories
.5 milligram cholesterol

Dissolve the arrowroot in the water in a saucepan and cook over medium heat, stirring constantly, until mixture comes to a boil. Continue stirring until clear and thickened, about 2 minutes. Remove the mixture from the saucepan to a bowl and place in refrigerator to chill.

Combine the white wine vinegar with salt and white pepper and stir until the salt and pepper have dissolved completely. Pour the vinegar in a small mixing bowl and using a wire whisk, mix the mustard into the vinegar. Slowly add the corn oil, continuing to mix the dressing with the wire whisk. Combine the milk with the arrowroot mixture and add to the dressing. Again, mix thoroughly with the wire whisk.

GREEN GOODNESS DRESSING

4 teaspoons arrowroot
1 cup water
1 cup plain, low-fat yogurt
1/2 cup safflower oil mayonnaise
1/2 teaspoon salt
dash of white pepper

1/4 cup tarragon vinegar
2 tablespoons dry white wine
  (I use Chablis)
1 cup finely chopped parsley
1/2 cup finely chopped chives or
  green onion tops
6 anchovy fillets, chopped

Makes 3 cups
Each 1/4 cup contains:
2 fat portions
90 calories
7.8 milligrams cholesterol

Dissolve arrowroot in 1/2 cup of cold water. Add the remaining 1/2 cup water and pour in a small saucepan. Bring to a slow boil over medium heat, stirring constantly until clear and thickened, about 2 or 3 minutes. Refrigerate arrowroot-water mixture until chilled.

While this mixture is chilling, prepare the remaining part of the dressing. Into a blender, put the yogurt and the mayonnaise, salt, pepper, vinegar and wine. Add the parsley, chives and anchovies to the other ingredients in the blender. Blend thoroughly. This will be a smooth, creamy thick liquid, pale green in color. Pour into a large mixing bowl. Add the chilled arrowroot-water mixture and mix thoroughly, using a wire whisk. Pour the dressing into a jar or container with a tight-fitting top. Keep refrigerated.

SIN-FREE SALAD DRESSING
(Low in Calories for a Clear Conscience)

3/4 cup unsweetened pineapple juice
3/4 cup tomato juice
1 tablespoon freshly squeezed lemon
  juice
sugar substitute = 1/4 teaspoon sugar
1/4 teaspoon salt

1 garlic bud, pressed
1/8 teaspoon freshly ground black
  pepper
1/8 teaspoon dry mustard
1 tablespoon pimiento, chopped
1 teaspoon capers, chopped

Makes 1-1/2 cups
Each tablespoon is:
Free food, calories negligible
0 cholesterol

Combine pineapple juice, tomato juice, lemon juice, sugar substitute and salt. Mix thoroughly until salt completely dissolves. Add all other ingredients and mix thoroughly. Store in a tightly covered container in the refrigerator. This is a divine salad dressing on all types of salad.

salads

Salads are my favorite form of food, so much so that I have often been accused of having a rabbit ancestry! For this reason, I tend to get carried away with the length of both my salad section and my cold, cooked vegetable section. In an attempt to make it easier to use the recipes in these sections, I have put the vegetables right after the salads and the cold, cooked vegetables in front of the cooked, hot ones. When looking through the salad section for an unusual starter course, always check the cold, cooked vegetable section also for such unusual first courses as Marinated Eggplant and Cucumbers Dilly Dilly. Both are excellent served as a salad course, as well as being good accompaniments to the meal itself.

Always try to wash salad greens several hours before you plan to serve them. Pat dry with paper towels and place in a colander so that any remaining moisture will drip through. Place the colander on a plate to catch the water and put in the refrigerator until ready to use. Not only will your salads be more crisp when the lettuce or other salad greens are completely dry, but you will need far less salad dressing to completely coat each leaf and, when calories are precious, the less dressing the better!

Chill your salad plates in the freezer. Salads should always be served on *very* cold plates.

salads

TROPICAL CHICKEN SALAD

1/2 cup pine nuts
6 cups shredded lettuce (1 large head)
3 cups chopped, cooked chicken
2 cups diced fresh pineapple or un-
    sweetened canned pineapple chunks
1 small papaya, peeled and diced, or

1 large apple, diced or navel orange,
    peeled and diced, if papaya is
    unavailable
1/2 cup Tropical Salad Dressing,
    page 54

Makes 6 servings

Each serving with dressing contains:
2 protein portions
1 fruit portion
3 fat portions
321 calories
44.8 milligrams cholesterol

Place pine nuts in 350° oven for 15 minutes, or until a golden brown in color. Cool before using.

Shred lettuce and wash thoroughly in colander, being sure the lettuce is *completely dry* before adding other ingredients. Combine lettuce with all other ingredients and toss thoroughly. This salad can either be served on large chilled plates garnished with parsley or sprigs of mint, or, for a more dramatic presentation, it can be served in hollowed-out pineapple halves using 2 cups of the fresh pineapple in the salad and saving the rest for another meal. I sometimes use 3 cups of pineapple, eliminating the second fruit when serving this salad in pineapple shells.

CHEF'S SALAD

1/2 head cabbage, finely chopped
1/2 head lettuce, finely chopped
1 large or 2 medium-size tomatoes,
    diced
1 cup crumbled farmer cheese

1 cup diced Monterey Jack cheese
2 cups diced cooked turkey or chicken
3/4 cup Happy Heart Dressing, page 48

Makes 8 servings

Each serving with dressing contains:
2 protein portions
2-1/4 fat portions
246 calories
43 milligrams cholesterol

Combine all ingredients and toss thoroughly with the dressing until the salad glistens. Serve on chilled plates. I suggest serving Herb Bread with this salad. It's a delicious combination!

VARIATION: Omit the tomatoes and add 2 large or 3 medium-size crisp red apples, diced, to this salad. If you do this, add 1 fruit portion and 40 calories to each serving.

TACO SALAD

1 head lettuce, finely chopped
1/2 pound ground sirloin of beef
2 large tomatoes, diced
1-1/2 cups grated Cheddar cheese

3/4 cup Happy Heart Cumin Dressing,
   page 50
3 tablespoons sour cream

Makes 6 servings

Each serving with dressing contains:
2 protein portions
2 fat portions
236 calories
60.4 milligrams cholesterol

Wash and chop lettuce in advance. Place lettuce in a colander so that all moisture can drip out of the lettuce before preparing the salad. Place colander in the refrigerator. Crumble the ground sirloin and cook over medium heat until just done.

Put the chopped lettuce, diced tomatoes, cooked, warm sirloin and 3/4 cup of the grated Cheddar cheese in a large mixing bowl. Add the Happy Heart Cumin Dressing and toss well. Divide the salad on 6 plates. Sprinkle remaining 3/4 cup of grated Cheddar cheese evenly on top of each serving. Put 1-1/2 teaspoons sour cream on top of each salad. I like to serve this with Toasted Tortilla Triangles.

HAPPY HEART CAESAR SALAD

2 heads Romaine lettuce (12 cups
   bite-size pieces)
2 cups Bread Croutons, page 122
2 tablespoons Garlic-Flavored Oil,
   page 47

2 tablespoons Parmesan cheese
1 cup Happy Heart Caesar
   Dressing, page 52

Makes 12 servings

Each serving with dressing contains:
1/4 starch portion
3 fat portions
152 calories
0 cholesterol

Several hours before serving, wash and dry the Romaine lettuce thoroughly. Tear it into bite-size pieces and put in a large bowl lined with a cloth to absorb any remaining moisture. Store in the refrigerator until ready to serve.

Put the croutons in a large jar with a tight-fitting lid. Add the Garlic-Flavored Oil and shake well. Then add the Parmesan cheese and shake again. When ready to serve, remove the cloth from under the lettuce and add the salad dressing. Toss the salad until every leaf glistens. Add the croutons and *again* toss thoroughly.

salads

ASTORIA SALAD

2 large, 3 medium, or 4 small chilled, unpeeled red apples, grated

4 stalks celery, without leaves, finely chopped

3 teaspoons Toasted Almond Flakes, page 45

2 tablespoons Happy Heart Dressing, page 48

Makes 4 servings

Each serving with dressing contains:
1 fruit portion
1 fat portion
85 calories
0 cholesterol

Toss all ingredients together until thoroughly mixed and serve immediately or apples will darken. This is a marvelous salad accompaniment to most poultry and holiday-type meals. I frequently use this recipe as a luncheon salad by adding leftover cold turkey or chicken.

CELERY ROOT SALAD

2 large celery roots (4 cups shredded)

2/3 cup Dijon Mustard Dressing, page 54

1/2 cup minced parsley

Makes 8 servings

Each serving with dressing contains:
1 B vegetable portion

1-1/2 fat portions
104 calories
5.2 milligrams cholesterol

Peel the celery root and shred using a grater or adjust a fluted blade of mandoline so that the blades are close enough to shred the celery root. Pour the dressing over the shredded celery root in a large mixing bowl and mix thoroughly. Serve on cold plates. Sprinkle top of each serving with minced parsley.

GREEK SALAD

2 cups finely chopped head lettuce
2 cups finely chopped raw cabbage
1 large tomato, diced
1 cup crumbled farmer cheese

1/2 cup Red Wine Vinegar Dressing,
   page 53

Makes 8 servings

Each serving with dressing contains:
1/2 protein portion
1-1/2 fat portions
105 calories
3 milligrams cholesterol

Toss all ingredients together, mixing thoroughly. Serve on chilled plates.

GAZPACHO PARTY MOLD

1 envelope unflavored gelatin
1-1/2 cups beef stock
1/4 cup red wine vinegar
1 teaspoon salt
1 teaspoon paprika
1/2 teaspoon sweet basil
1/8 teaspoon ground cloves

1/8 teaspoon Tabasco sauce
1 garlic bud, minced
2 tablespoons minced onion
1/4 cup finely chopped celery
1/2 cup peeled and finely chopped
   cucumber

1/2 cup seeded and finely chopped
   green bell pepper
2 large tomatoes, peeled and chopped
fresh parsley or cilantro for garnish

Makes 6 servings
Free food, calories negligible
0 cholesterol

Sprinkle the gelatin over 1/4 cup of the cold beef stock. Bring the remaining 1-1/4 cups of beef stock to a boil and add the gelatin and beef stock mixture, stirring until gelatin is dissolved. Cool to room temperature. Add the vinegar, seasonings and garlic. Chill until mixture is slightly thickened. Fold in all remaining vegetables and pour into an oiled 4-cup ring mold. Chill until firm and turn onto a serving plate. Garnish with fresh parsley or cilantro. This can be chilled in soup cups for individual servings and makes a marvelous and very unusual soup course.

salads

CRANBERRY-APPLE HOLIDAY WREATH SALAD

4 large (or 6 small) red apples, peeled, cored and diced
1-1/2 tablespoons freshly squeezed lemon juice
4 cups water
sugar substitute = 1 cup sugar
1 teaspoon ground cinnamon
1-1/2 tablespoons vanilla extract

5 drops red food coloring
1 pound (4 cups) fresh or frozen, unsweetened cranberries
2 envelopes unflavored gelatin
1/2 cup boiling water
1-1/2 cups low-fat milk
1/2 cup low-fat plain yogurt
1/2 cup dry white wine (I like Chablis)
watercress or parsley sprigs

Makes 12 servings
Each serving contains:
1/2 fruit portion
20 calories
2.7 milligrams cholesterol

Peel, core and dice the apples. Sprinkle the diced apples with the lemon juice and set aside. In a large saucepan, combine the 4 cups water, sugar substitute, cinnamon, vanilla and red food coloring. Bring mixture to a boil. Reduce the heat and simmer for 5 minutes. Add the cranberries to the simmering liquid and cook for 10 minutes. Add the apples to the cranberries and cook together for 10 more minutes. Remove from heat and cool to room temperature. Refrigerate until cold. If possible, allow the cranberries and apples to marinate overnight in the poaching liquid.

Remove from the refrigerator and drain the poaching liquid from the cranberry-apple mixture, reserving 1/2 cup of this liquid. Add the gelatin to the 1/2 cup cold poaching liquid and allow it to soften for at least 5 minutes. Then add 1/2 cup boiling water to the gelatin mixture and stir until the gelatin is completely dissolved.

Put the cranberry-apple mixture in the blender. Add the poaching liquid and as much of the milk as necessary to purée the cranberries and apples. When the mixture is a liquid consistency, pour it into a large mixing bowl and add the remaining milk, yogurt and white wine. Mix thoroughly, using a wire whisk. Pour the entire mixture into a large oiled ring mold. Chill for several hours or, preferably, overnight before unmolding. To unmold, tap the bottom and sides of the mold with the handle of a knife. Place a large plate over the mold and invert quickly. Garnish with fresh watercress or parsley for a touch of holiday greenery. This makes a beautiful and colorful holiday salad.

BETTY'S SAUERKRAUT SALAD

2 cups well-drained sauerkraut
1/2 cup grated carrots
1-1/2 cups minced celery
1-1/2 cups seeded and chopped
   green bell pepper

1/2 cup seeded and chopped
   sweet red pepper
1/2 cup finely chopped onions
1/3 cup white vinegar
sugar substitute = 1/2 cup sugar
1 teaspoon salt
dash of freshly ground black pepper

Makes 12 1/2-cup servings
Each 1/2 cup serving is:
Free food, calories negligible
0 cholesterol

Put sauerkraut in colander and rinse with cold water. Allow to drain thoroughly. Combine sauerkraut with all other ingredients. Refrigerate all day or preferably overnight before serving.

vegetables cold and hot

Many people do not take full advantage of the wide variety of exciting and unusual uses vegetables can offer in the imaginative and healthy diet. For instance, cold, cooked vegetables are too often literally "left out in the cold" and eventually thrown out as unwanted leftovers. Many of the glamorous and unique vegetable dishes are first cooked and then chilled. Asparagus Vinaigrette is my favorite appetizer and, when fresh asparagus is either not in season or too expensive, Celery Root Vinaigrette is a great second choice. Your friends will "rave" over your Cucumbers Dilly Dilly and ask for seconds of your Marinated Mushrooms!

The hot vegetables can often be "the star of the plate." If you don't believe this, just try serving your steamed peas in onion cups, or fill a crown roast of lamb with Minted Carrots. Another great use of vegetables is for a vegetarian entrée, such as Broccoli and Cheese Casserole or Italian Carrot Classic.

CUCUMBERS DILLY DILLY

3 large cucumbers
salt
1/2 cup Sauce Dilly Dilly, page 44
sugar substitute = 1/8 teaspoon sugar

dash of freshly ground black pepper
1/8 teaspoon freshly squeezed lemon
 juice

Makes 8 servings

Each serving contains:
1 fat portion
45 calories
3 milligrams cholesterol

Peel the cucumbers, and using the slot for thinly sliced vegetables of a four-sided grater, slice the cucumbers into paper-thin rounds. Place the sliced cucumbers in a non-metal bowl and sprinkle generously with salt, mixing thoroughly. Cover the bowl and place it in the refrigerator for at least 3 hours. After 3 hours (or longer won't hurt them), put the cucumbers in a strainer or colander and place them under cold running water until thoroughly washed. Keep mixing the cucumber slices to allow the salt to be washed off all of them. Press as much of the remaining water out of the colander as possible with your hand. Then, dump all of the cucumbers out on towels and pat them with another towel or paper towels until they are completely dry. At this point, the thin cucumber slices will be very limp. Put them in a bowl. Mix the Sauce Dilly Dilly with the sugar substitute, pepper and lemon juice and pour over the cucumbers. Mix thoroughly.

These cucumbers are a fabulous accompaniment to cold poached salmon or any cold seafood. Also, they are nice served as an appetizer on lettuce leaves before a fish or seafood meal. When I serve them as a salad, I garnish the top with a bit of minced parsley.

vegetables cold and hot

PICNIC PICKLES

1 quart kosher dill pickles
sugar substitute = 1 cup sugar

1 teaspoon mustard seed
2 garlic buds, cut in half

Makes 1 quart
Free food, calories negligible
0 cholesterol

Drain all juice from the pickles, keeping the jar. Slice the pickles crosswise in 1/2-inch slices. Put the pickle slices in a bowl and mix thoroughly with sugar substitute and mustard seed.

Put the pickles back in the jar and add the halved garlic buds. Put the lid on the jar tightly and shake vigorously. Allow to stand several days in the refrigerator before serving. Turn the jar from side to side several times each day.

PICNIC PICKLE RELISH

1 cup Picnic Pickles, preceding
1 2-ounce jar pimientos

Makes 1-1/4 cups

Free food, calories negligible
0 cholesterol

Finely chop together pickles and pimientos. Serve on hamburgers or as desired.

PICKLED ONION RELISH

2-1/2 pounds Spanish onions (4
   large onions)
1-1/2 cups cider vinegar
1 garlic bud, halved

sugar substitute = 1 cup sugar
1/8 teaspoon pickling spices, crushed

Makes approximately 3 cups

Each 1/2 cup contains:
1 B vegetable portion
36 calories
0 cholesterol

Peel the onions and, using the slicing section of a grater, slice them into very thin slices. Separate the slices into lengths and parboil for 1 minute; drain thoroughly. Combine all other ingredients in a non-metal bowl and add the onions to the mixture. Press the onions down into the marinade with the back of a wooden spoon. Cover and allow to stand at room temperature for 24 hours, stirring occasionally. Store in the refrigerator in a sealed glass container.

This onion relish has long been a favorite in my family as a cold meat accompaniment. Also, I like to sprinkle a spoonful or so over the top of some salads.

ASPARAGUS VINAIGRETTE

20 fresh asparagus spears
1 cup Happy Heart Vinaigrette
    Dressing, page 49

1 2-ounce jar sliced pimientos
1/4 cup capers

Makes 4 servings

Each serving contains:
1 fat portion
45 calories
0 cholesterol

Thoroughly wash asparagus and break off tough end sections. Place asparagus spears in steamer and steam for about 8 minutes, or until tender crisp but not limp. Cool asparagus to room temperature and place in a glass baking dish, all pointing in the same direction. (This makes removing them for serving much simpler.) Pour the Happy Heart Vinaigrette Dressing over the asparagus and cover tightly with foil. Refrigerate all day or overnight to thoroughly marinate the asparagus. To serve, place in chilled asparagus dishes or salad plates and place the pimiento strips and capers equally over each serving. I often serve this as a first course, omitting salad.

MARINATED EGGPLANT
(Appetizer or Salad)

1 medium-size firm eggplant
salt
1 cup Happy Heart Cumin Dressing,
    page 50

1 large ripe tomato, peeled and diced
1 large onion, peeled and diced
1/2 cup finely minced parsley

Makes 6 servings

Each serving contains:
1-1/2 fat portions
68 calories
0 cholesterol

Peel eggplant and slice in 1/4-inch slices. Spread the eggplant slices in a glass baking dish, sprinkling both sides with salt. Cover and allow to stand for at least 1 hour. Pour off liquid. Place eggplant in a steamer and steam until just fork tender. Be careful not to overcook to a mushy texture. Place the steamed eggplant back in the glass baking dish and pour the dressing over it. Allow eggplant to cool to room temperature. Cover and refrigerate for 2 to 3 hours. One hour before serving the eggplant, add the tomatoes and onion and allow to marinate in the dressing. Serve on chilled plates, topped with the tomato and onion garnish. Sprinkle parsley over entire dish. This is a deliciously different and easily served cold vegetable for buffets.

vegetables cold and hot

MARINATED MUSHROOMS

1 pound large fresh mushrooms
2 cups red wine vinegar
1/2 cup Happy Heart Tarragon
   Dressing, page 48
1/4 cup finely minced parsley

Each mushroom contains approximately:
1/2 fat portion
23 calories
0 cholesterol

When buying fresh mushrooms, make certain you get those with tightly closed caps. This indicates very fresh mushrooms. When the caps open, the mushrooms tend to be dry and tough. Wash mushrooms and dry thoroughly. Slice vertically in about 1/4-inch slices. Put mushroom slices in a jar or non-metal container and pour the red wine vinegar over them. If the vinegar does not cover the mushrooms, add more vinegar to cover. Cover the container and allow to stand at room temperature for 1 hour. Remove the mushrooms from the vinegar and arrange decoratively on a large platter or serving dish. Sprinkle the mushrooms evenly with the Happy Heart Tarragon Dressing. Sprinkle the minced parsley evenly on the top. Cover the platter with foil or saran wrap and place in the refrigerator for at least 3 hours before serving.

This may be used either as an hors d'oeuvre served with toothpicks to pick up the mushroom slices, as a cold vegetable plate for a buffet using a salad serving fork to place the mushrooms on individual plates, or you may use the mushrooms to garnish your own individual salads of various types. This platter would make hors d'oeuvre for at least 24 people.

vegetables cold and hot

DUTCH BROCCOLI

2 pounds fresh broccoli (4 stalks)
3/4 cup Simple Hollandaise Sauce,
  page 42

Makes 8 servings
Each serving contains:

3 fat portions
135 calories
6 milligrams cholesterol

Wash broccoli thoroughly. Chop off the end stem, usually about 1-1/2 inches. Coarsely chop all of the broccoli and steam for about 7 minutes, or until tender crisp. (This particular dish is not good if the broccoli is soft, because it then becomes mushy.) Remove the broccoli to a large bowl. Add the Hollandaise sauce and toss until thoroughly mixed. This dish is best served immediately. However, when time is a problem, it can be made ahead and then reheated in a 350° oven for about 15 minutes. It can be served cold, also, as a vegetable salad.

BROCCOLI AND CHEESE CASSEROLE

2 pounds fresh broccoli (about 4 cups
  steamed and chopped)
4 teaspoons corn oil
1/4 cup minced onion
2-1/2 tablespoons flour
1/2 cup boiling water

1/2 teaspoon salt
1 cup grated sharp Cheddar cheese
1 cup crumbled farmer cheese
1 4-ounce jar pimientos, chopped
1 egg white, beaten stiff but not dry

Makes 6 servings
Each serving contains:
1-1/2 protein portions
1/2 fat portion
133 calories
33.1 milligrams cholesterol

Wash broccoli and *trim carefully,* cutting off fibrous ends and tough outer leaves. Steam for about 8 minutes (you should be able to pierce the broccoli stem with a fork but it should feel crisp to the touch). Cool broccoli until it can be easily handled and chop coarsely.

Put corn oil in a large saucepan and warm over medium heat. Add minced onion and cook, stirring, until clear, about 4 minutes. Add flour and cook, stirring constantly, about 3 minutes. *Do not allow flour to brown.* Add boiling water and salt and stir until slightly thickened. Add cheeses and stir until they melt. Add pimiento to cheese mixture and mix thoroughly. Combine the cheese mixture and chopped broccoli. Mix together thoroughly. Add the beaten egg white and again mix thoroughly. Pour the mixture in a casserole and bake, uncovered, in a 350° oven for 45 minutes.

ITALIAN CARROT CLASSIC

3 tablespoons corn oil margarine
2 garlic buds, minced
1 pound carrots (8 small), peeled
   and grated
1 cup minced onion
1/4 cup minced parsley
2 cups Italian tomatoes, peeled and
   chopped (1 20-ounce can)

1 6-ounce can tomato paste
1 teaspoon oregano
1/4 teaspoon sweet basil
1/2 teaspoon salt
1/4 teaspoon freshly ground
   black pepper
3-1/2 cups grated Mozzarella cheese
1/2 cup grated Parmesan cheese

Makes 8 servings
Each serving contains:
2 protein portions
1 fat portion
1 group B vegetable portion
227 calories
27.2 milligrams cholesterol

Heat the margarine in a large skillet. Add the garlic and carrots and cook together over medium heat, stirring occasionally, for 10 minutes. Add the minced onion and parsley and continue cooking for another 10 minutes. Add the tomatoes, tomato paste, oregano, basil, salt and pepper and simmer uncovered for 30 minutes longer.

Spoon one-half of the vegetable mixture into a large casserole. Add half of the grated Mozzarella cheese and half of the Parmesan cheese. Add the remaining vegetables and the remaining Mozzarella cheese. Sprinkle the Parmesan cheese evenly over the top of the casserole. Place in a 350° oven and bake, uncovered, for 30 minutes.

MINTED CARROTS

1 pound carrots (8 small)
2 teaspoons arrowroot
1/2 cup water
2 tablespoons corn oil margarine

1/2 teaspoon salt
sugar substitute = 1 teaspoon sugar
1/2 cup minced fresh mint leaves

Makes 8 servings

Each serving contains:
1 B vegetable portion
3/4 fat portion
48 calories
0 cholesterol

Scrape outside skin from carrots carefully and slice in 1/4-inch rounds. Using a steamer above boiling water, steam carrots until they are tender crisp. Be careful not to overcook them as it gives them a mushy consistency. Dissolve arrowroot in water and cook, stirring constantly, over medium heat until mixture comes to a boil. Stir until it is clear and thickened, about 2 minutes. Remove from heat and add margarine, salt and sugar substitute and mix thoroughly. Pour over the steamed carrots. Add fresh mint and toss, mixing all ingredients thoroughly.

VARIATION: This recipe is also delicious made with steamed green peas.

vegetables cold and hot

FANCY FRENCH-CUT GREEN STRING BEANS

1 tablespoon corn oil margarine

2 medium onions, peeled and thinly
sliced

2 pounds fresh green string beans (if
not available, use 3 packages of
frozen French-cut green string
beans)

1-1/2 cups Basic White Sauce, page 38

2 tablespoons soy sauce

1 6-ounce can water chestnuts,
thinly sliced

Makes 8 servings

Each serving contains:
3/4 fat portion
1/4 milk portion
1/2 B vegetable portion
83 calories
4 milligrams cholesterol

Heat margarine in a cured heavy iron skillet. Add the onions and cook until well browned. Remove all strings from the green beans and slice diagonally into 1/4-inch strips. Steam the beans over simmering water until tender crisp, about 8 to 10 minutes.

Mix the Basic White Sauce and soy sauce together thoroughly. Combine the browned onions, steamed beans and water chestnuts. Add the white sauce mixture and mix thoroughly. Put the entire bean mixture in a casserole and bake, uncovered, in a 325° oven for 1 hour.

VARIATION: This makes an excellent main course by adding 2 7-ounce cans of tuna, drained and mixed with the bean mixture before placing it in the oven. Add to each serving: 1 protein portion, 73 calories and 36.7 milligrams cholesterol.

SPINACH SURPRISE

3 pounds fresh spinach, coarsely
    chopped (3 cups cooked)
1 cup finely chopped onion
4 teaspoons powdered beef stock base
1/4 cup dry white wine (I use Chablis)

1 cup low-fat cottage cheese
1/2 cup low-fat plain yogurt
2 egg whites, beaten stiff but not dry

Makes 8 servings

Each serving contains:
1/2 protein portion
1/4 B vegetable portion
46 calories
2.4 milligrams cholesterol

Carefully wash spinach and break off tough ends. Coarsely chop. Steam chopped spinach for about 2 minutes and drain well. Heat a cured heavy iron skillet; wipe with corn oil. Put onion in skillet and cook over low heat for 30 minutes, until onion is soft and brown. Dissolve beef stock base in the wine. Turn heat up high under onion and stir constantly. Add the wine, cooking 2 to 3 minutes, or until the moisture is absorbed. Remove skillet from heat and put the drained spinach in the skillet with the onion, mixing thoroughly. Combine the cottage cheese and yogurt and add to spinach mixture. Beat the egg whites and fold into the spinach mixture. Pour entire mixture into a casserole or baking dish and bake, uncovered, at 350° for 35 minutes.

SWEET & SOUR RED CABBAGE

1 small head (or 1/2 large one) red
    cabbage
1/2 cup water
2 teaspoons arrowroot

1/2 cup cider vinegar
sugar substitute = 3 tablespoons sugar
1/8 teaspoon salt
1/2 teaspoon caraway seeds

Makes 8 servings
Free food, calories negligible
0 cholesterol

Shred cabbage and steam over boiling water for 15 minutes, or until tender crisp. While cabbage is cooking, dissolve the arrowroot in the 1/2 cup water and cook over medium heat until clear and thickened. Remove from heat and add the vinegar, sugar substitute, salt and caraway seeds, mixing thoroughly. Remove steamed cabbage and place in a mixing bowl. Pour the sauce over the cabbage and toss, mixing thoroughly.

vegetables cold and hot

CAULIFLOWER BOUQUET

1 large head of cauliflower
3 cups chicken stock
2 tablespoons freshly squeezed
    lemon juice

1-1/2 teaspoons oregano
1/2 teaspoon sweet basil
freshly ground black pepper

Makes 6 servings
Without topping free food,
    calories negligible
0 cholesterol

Select the largest, whitest, most beautiful head of cauliflower you can find. Carefully remove all green outer leaves at the base of the cauliflower. Cut off stems as closely as possible and then cut into the stalk, removing cone-shaped section of stem from the inside of the center of the cauliflower. This allows both heat and flavor to penetrate through the entire head.

Put stock in a large kettle. Place cauliflower on a large sheet of aluminum foil and lower into kettle. This will enable you to remove the cauliflower without breaking it when it is cooked. Sprinkle the lemon juice evenly over cauliflower. Using a mortar and pestle, crush the oregano and basil together thoroughly and then sprinkle evenly over cauliflower along with a touch of freshly ground pepper. Cook for approximately 30 minutes or until easily pierced with a fork, but not soft. Carefully lift the cooked cauliflower from the cooking stock by lifting the 4 corners of the aluminum foil. Serve on a large round platter and cover with Tomato Cheese Topping or any other sauce of your choice.

74

SUN-KISSED SQUASH

1/2 cup finely chopped walnuts
4 oranges
3 pounds banana or winter squash, or
3 16-ounce packages frozen winter
  squash
1/4 cup freshly squeezed orange juice
1 teaspoon grated orange peel

2 teaspoons vanilla extract
1 teaspoon ground cinnamon
1/4 teaspoon ground nutmeg
liquid egg substitute = 1 egg
1/2 cup low-fat milk
2 teaspoons corn oil margarine, melted
1/2 cup seedless raisins

Makes 8 servings
Each serving contains:
1/2 B vegetable portion
1/2 fruit portion
1 fat portion
83 calories
9 milligrams cholesterol

Put the walnuts in a 350° oven for approximately 15 minutes, or until well toasted. Set aside to add as last ingredient. To make orange cups, slice 4 oranges in half horizontally. Remove *all* pulp. (You can serve sliced oranges for breakfast that day!) If you wish, scallop the top of each orange cup for a fancier presentation.

If you use fresh squash, first peel the squash and cut it into approximately 1-inch cubes. Steam until fork tender. Place in large mixing bowl, cool slightly and then mash. If using frozen, cooked squash, place the completely thawed squash in a large mixing bowl. Add to the squash the orange juice and the grated orange peel, being careful to use only the orange part of the peel, as the white part has a bitter taste. Add the vanilla, cinnamon and nutmeg to the squash. Combine the egg substitute with the milk and add to the squash. Beat the squash mixture with an electric mixer or rotary hand beater until fluffy. Melt the margarine and add to mixture, continuing beating until thoroughly mixed. Fold in the raisins and chopped, toasted walnuts and mix thoroughly. Pour the entire mixture into an ovenproof casserole and bake, uncovered, in a 325° oven for 30 minutes.

If you are making this in advance, do not bake until you are ready to serve it. Cover tightly and store in the refrigerator. Remove 2 to 3 hours before cooking so that it will come to room temperature before baking.

vegetables cold and hot

TEXAS TURNIPS

8 medium-size turnips
1 tablespoon imitation bacon bits
1/2 teaspoon salt
sugar substitute = 1 teaspoon sugar

1/4 teaspoon freshly ground
  black pepper
additional 1/2 teaspoon salt

Makes 6 1/2-cup servings

Each 1/2 cup contains:
1 B vegetable portion
36 calories
1 milligram cholesterol

Peel and slice turnips. In a saucepan put the turnips, bacon bits and salt and cover with water. Cook until soft. Drain water from turnips and mash turnips with a potato masher adding the sugar substitute, pepper and salt. Continue mashing until well mixed. This is a delightfully different way to present a group B vegetable.

RAVABLE RUTABAGAS

6 medium-size rutabagas, peeled and
  diced
2 cups green bell peppers, finely
  chopped
3 cups chicken stock
1-1/2 teaspoons chervil

1/4 teaspoon freshly ground
  black pepper
1/2 cup minced parsley
1/2 cup grated Monterey Jack cheese

Makes 8 servings

Each serving contains:
1 B vegetable portion
1/4 protein portion
54 calories
4.5 milligrams cholesterol

In a covered pot, cook rutabagas and green pepper in the chicken stock over medium heat, until vegetables are soft and easily pierced with a fork (about 25 minutes). Drain the vegetables and mash them with a potato masher. Add remaining ingredients and mix thoroughly. Put the mashed mixture in a covered casserole and bake in a 350° oven for 40 minutes. Even people who swear they *won't* eat rutabagas will rave about this unusual vegetable!

CREAMED MUSHROOMS

1 pound fresh mushrooms	Makes 2 cups	1/4 milk portion
1 tablespoon corn oil margarine	Each 1/4 cup contains:	66 calories
2 tablespoons Sherry	3/4 fat portion	2.5 milligrams cholesterol
1 cup Basic White Sauce, page 38		

Thoroughly wash and dry the mushrooms. Slice off the top stem ends and discard. Finely chop the mushrooms. Melt the margarine in a large cured heavy iron skillet. Add the mushrooms and cook over medium heat, stirring frequently, until the mushrooms are tender (about 20 minutes). Add the Sherry, increase the heat slightly, and cook, stirring continuously, until liquid is reduced by one-half. Remove the mushrooms from the heat and add the white sauce, stirring thoroughly.

The creamed mushrooms may be served immediately or refrigerated to be used later. This is a fabulous recipe used as a vegetable with your entrée, or as a filling for crêpes, omelets or other vegetables; or try it as a sauce over fish, poultry or meat. I even use it as a sauce over cheese soufflés for a divine brunch dish. Try it! Surely you will find some new imaginative way of serving it.

CREAMED CELERY ROOT

2 medium-size celery roots (or 1 very large)	dash of white pepper	Each serving contains:
	1 drop yellow food coloring	1 B vegetable portion
1 cup buttermilk		36 calories
3/4 teaspoon salt	Makes 6 servings	1.3 milligrams cholesterol

Peel the celery roots and dice into 1/2-inch cubes. Put the cubes in a steamer and steam for about 10 minutes, or until tender enough to mash. Remove the celery root from the steamer and reserve 1/2 cup of liquid. Put the liquid and part of the cooked celery roots in a blender. Slowly and alternately add the buttermilk and the remaining cooked celery root. Add the salt, pepper and food coloring and blend at high speed 2 or 3 minutes until a velvety consistency. This is one of my favorite vegetables, particularly when served with any meat, fish or poultry dish containing tomato.

vegetables cold and hot

PINE NUT PILAF

1/2 cup pine nuts
1 cup long-grain white rice
4 teaspoons corn oil
1/2 cup minced onion
2 cups chicken stock

1/4 teaspoon ground nutmeg
1/4 teaspoon sage

Makes 8 1/2-cup servings

Each 1/2 cup serving contains:
1 starch portion
1-1/2 fat portions
136 calories
0 cholesterol

Place pine nuts in a 350° oven for 15 minutes, or until a golden brown in color. Spread the uncooked rice in a heavy iron skillet and place in a 400° oven. Stir frequently until golden brown in color, about 12 to 15 minutes. Put rice in another container to cool.

Heat the corn oil in a cured heavy iron skillet. Add the onion and browned rice. Cook, stirring frequently, until the rice is opaque and the onion cooked, about 15 minutes. Add the nutmeg and sage to the chicken stock and combine with the rice and onion. Cook until mixture begins to simmer. Remove from heat, add the pine nuts and mix thoroughly. Pour entire mixture into a casserole with tight-fitting lid. Place in a 350° oven for 25 minutes. Remove from the oven and leave covered for 10 minutes before removing lid. (You can actually leave the lid on much longer than this if you want to wait for another part of the meal to be ready, as the rice will stay hot for quite a long time.)

VARIATION: This recipe is also good with raisins. I like to use 1/2 cup of raisins, which will add to each 1/2 cup serving: 1/2 fruit portion, 20 calories, 0 cholesterol.

MYSTERY PILAF

1/2 cup uncooked vermicelli, broken
   in 1-inch pieces
3 tablespoons corn oil
1 cup long-grain white rice

1/2 medium-size onion, thinly sliced
2 cups chicken stock
2 tablespoons soy sauce
1 teaspoon thyme

Makes 12 1/2-cup servings

Each 1/2 cup serving contains:
1 starch portion
3/4 fat portion
102 calories
0 cholesterol

Put vermicelli on a cookie sheet with sides or in a baking dish. Place in a 400° oven and stir occasionally, until a rich brown in color.

Heat the oil in a cured heavy iron skillet and add the rice and onion slices to the heated oil. Cook, stirring frequently, until browned thoroughly.

Add the browned vermicelli, soy sauce and thyme to the chicken stock and bring to the boiling point. Put the rice mixture in a casserole dish with a tight-fitting lid and add the hot stock. Stir and cover. Place in a 400° oven for 40 minutes. Remove from the oven and allow to stand for 10 minutes before removing lid. To reheat: Add 2 or 3 tablespoons of chicken stock to the cold rice and mix thoroughly. Cover and heat slowly in a 300° oven for about 15 minutes.

vegetables cold and hot

ORIENTAL VEGETABLES

1 teaspoon corn oil
1 medium-size onion, thinly sliced
2 cups fresh pea pods (if fresh ones
   not available, use frozen)

1 6-ounce can water chestnuts,
   thinly sliced
1 cup bean sprouts
2 tablespoons soy sauce

Makes 8 servings

Each serving contains:
1 B vegetable portion
36 calories
0 cholesterol

In a cured heavy iron skillet, heat the corn oil and add the onion. Cook over medium heat for 3 to 5 minutes until tender crisp. Add the pea pods, water chestnuts, bean sprouts and soy sauce. Cook 3 to 5 minutes until pea pods are tender crisp.

RATATOUILLE

4 large tomatoes, cut in chunks
2 large (or 3 small) garlic buds, minced
1/2 cup minced parsley
1 teaspoon sweet basil, crushed using
   mortar and pestle
2 teaspoons salt
2 large onions, sliced

6 medium-size zucchini, sliced in
   1/2-inch rounds
2 green bell peppers, seeded and
   cut into 1/2-inch squares
1 medium-size eggplant, unpeeled and
   cut in 1/2-inch cubes
2 tablespoons corn oil

Makes 12 servings
Each serving contains:
1/2 fat portion
23 calories
0 cholesterol

Put tomatoes in large mixing bowl and add the garlic, parsley, sweet basil and salt, mixing well. Add remaining vegetables and, again, mix well. Place mixture in a 6-quart casserole with a cover, or in 2 3-quart casseroles with covers. Drip the corn oil over the top. Cover and place in a 350° oven for 3 hours. During the first 2 hours, baste top occasionally with some of the liquid to insure even flavoring. During the last hour of cooking uncover the casserole(s). Serve hot from the oven, or cool to room temperature and refrigerate. The flavor of this dish greatly improves if it is chilled and then reheated for serving. It may also be served cold. I like it best served cold either as an hors d'oeuvre or appetizer course.

vegetables cold and hot

BOUILLON BAKED SPANISH ONIONS

4 large Spanish onions, peeled
   and halved, or
24 small boiling onions, peeled and
   left whole
2 cups beef stock

dash of white pepper
1 teaspoon thyme
2 bay leaves
1/4 cup minced parsley

Makes 8 servings

Each serving contains:
1 B vegetable portion
36 calories
0 cholesterol

Place the onions in a single layer in a baking dish just large enough to hold them. Combine the stock, white pepper, thyme and mix thoroughly. Pour over the onions. Add the bay leaves whole, so you can easily remove them. Sprinkle minced parsley over the top. Cover tightly with lid or aluminum foil and place in a 325° oven for 35 minutes. Then cook for 10 more minutes, uncovered, allowing the stock to reduce. Remove bay leaves and serve. These onions are marvelous with all types of meat, fish and poultry. I even like them cold, chopped up in salads!

VARIATION: When using large onions, I usually make onion cups out of this recipe by removing the centers and refrigerating them for future use and serving another vegetable such as tiny peas in the cups. You can also chill the onion cups and use them for serving chopped cold meats.

PINEAPPLE-PUMPKIN PUFF

3-1/2 cups cooked and mashed fresh
   pumpkin, or
1 29-ounce can solid-pack
   pumpkin
1 cup crushed unsweetened pineapple
1 cup buttermilk

1 teaspoon ground cinnamon
1/4 teaspoon ground nutmeg
sugar substitute = 1 tablespoon sugar
2 teaspoons vanilla extract
1 egg white, beaten stiff but not dry

Makes 12 servings
Each serving contains:
1 B vegetable portion
36 calories
.7 milligram cholesterol

Put 1 cup of the pumpkin, all the pineapple, 1/2 cup of the buttermilk, cinnamon, nutmeg, sugar substitute and vanilla in a blender. Blend until smooth. Slowly add the remaining pumpkin and the remaining 1/2 cup of buttermilk and blend again until smooth. Pour pumpkin-pineapple mixture in a large casserole, fold in beaten egg white and bake, uncovered, in a 325° oven for 45 minutes.

eggs, egg substitutes and cheese

There was a time when mentioning an egg and a happy heart in the same breath was taboo! But now that modern technology has brought us the egg substitutes, our hearts can gaily go "pit-a-pat" when we see the soufflé billowing over the dish without *one* single egg yolk in it! Egg substitutes are much more believable as eggs when "jazzed-up" with an imaginative preparation. Therefore, if you are an "egg fancier," this is a particularly valuable chapter. There are several brands of egg substitutes on the market. I personally prefer to use the lower calorie substitutes which have only 50 calories per egg equivalent. Some of the popular brands have 100 calories per egg equivalent. Since most heart diets are also calorie-counting diets, the saving of 50 calories becomes important. Because red meats are restricted in the heart diet and because many vegetarians are also in need of happier hearts, egg substitutes are truly a blessing!

Egg yolks are not "all that bad." One egg yolk contains 250 milligrams of cholesterol, but, if you are allowed only 300 milligrams for the entire day, it does give reason for thought before indulging in one whole egg at a time. When using egg yolks, spread them out over several servings as I do in my recipe, Cinnamon Soufflé, in the dessert section. Each serving contains only 44.6 milligrams cholesterol, and can easily be used in even very low cholesterol diets.

Many cheeses are also quite high in cholesterol, but I like cheese so much myself, that I tend to save up most of the grams of cholesterol allowed in the weekly diets and use them for cheese! Fortunately, there are many new low-fat, low-cholesterol cheese-food products on the market. Many of them are excellent substitutes for popular favorites, such as, Cheddar, Swiss, Parmesan and Mozzarella. However, not all brands are available in all states. Check with your own market manager as to what is available in your area.

eggs, egg substitutes and cheese

CHICKEN CURRY SOUFFLÉ

1 cup low-fat milk	1/2 teaspoon salt	Makes 4 servings
4 teaspoons corn oil margarine	1/8 teaspoon white pepper	Each serving contains:
1/2 cup minced onion	1 cup chopped cooked chicken	2 protein portions
2-1/2 tablespoons all-purpose flour	4 egg whites at room temperature	1/4 milk portion
liquid egg substitute = 2 eggs	1/8 teaspoon cream of tartar	177 calories
2 teaspoons curry powder	pinch of salt	26 milligrams cholesterol

Preheat oven to 400°. Put milk in a saucepan on low heat and bring to boiling point. Put margarine in another large saucepan. Melt the margarine and add the onion. Cook over medium heat, stirring frequently, until the onion is soft. Add the flour and cook, stirring constantly, for 3 minutes. *Do not brown.*

Take the flour mixture off the heat and pour in the boiling milk all at once, stirring with a wire whisk. Put pan back on heat and allow to come to a boil, stirring constantly. Boil for 1 to 2 minutes. At this point the sauce will thicken slightly. Remove from heat. Add the egg substitute slowly, stirring constantly with wire whisk. Add curry powder, salt and pepper and mix thoroughly. Add the chicken and set aside while beating the egg whites. Add the cream of tartar and pinch of salt to egg whites and beat until stiff but not dry. Add one-fourth of the egg whites to the soufflé, mix and stir them in. Add the remaining egg whites to the soufflé and carefully fold them in, being sure not to overmix!

Pour the mixture into an 8-inch soufflé dish. Place it in the center of the oven which has been preheated to 400°. *Immediately* turn down the oven to 375°. Cook 25 minutes. Serve at once.

SOUFFLÉ OLÉ

2 tablespoons corn oil margarine
1/2 cup minced onion
1 large tomato, peeled and diced
1-1/2 teaspoons cumin
2-1/2 tablespoons flour
1 cup chicken stock, boiling
1/4 teaspoon salt

1/2 teaspoon chili powder
liquid egg substitute = 2 eggs
1 cup grated Monterey Jack cheese
1 4-ounce can green chilies, seeded
   and chopped
6 egg whites at room temperature
1/8 teaspoon cream of tartar
dash of salt

Makes 6 servings
Each serving contains:
2 protein portions
146 calories
12 milligrams cholesterol

Preheat oven to 400°. Melt margarine in a heavy saucepan large enough to hold the entire soufflé prior to putting it in the soufflé dish. Add the onion, tomato and cumin and cook over medium heat for 10 minutes, or until onion is soft and clear. Add flour and mix thoroughly. Cook for 3 minutes stirring constantly. Do not brown. Remove from heat and add the boiling stock all at once, rapidly mixing with a wire whisk to form a smooth mixture. Place back over medium heat and simmer for 3 to 4 minutes. When mixture has thickened remove from heat and add salt and chili powder. Slowly add egg substitute, stirring constantly as it is added. Add the grated cheese and chilies, mixing thoroughly. Add the cream of tartar and salt to the egg whites and beat until stiff but not dry. Mix one-quarter of the egg whites into the soufflé base to lighten it. Fold in the remaining egg whites, being careful not to overmix. Put the entire mixture into an 8-1/2-inch soufflé dish and place in middle of the oven and cook for 30 minutes. Remove from the oven and serve *immediately.*

I like to serve this soufflé with hot tortillas and tossed green salad with Red Wine Vinegar Dressing. For leftovers, it is excellent reheated and used for a vegetarian taco filling. Add shredded lettuce and diced tomatoes and a little taco sauce—olé! olé!

eggs, egg substitutes and cheese

TUNA SOUFFLÉ

1/2 cup low-fat milk
1/2 cup chicken stock
2 tablespoons corn oil margarine
1 tablespoon minced onion
2-1/2 tablespoons flour
2 egg yolks
1/4 teaspoon salt

1/8 teaspoon white pepper
1/4 teaspoon Worcestershire sauce
1/2 cup grated Cheddar cheese
1 7-ounce can tuna
8 egg whites at room temperature
1/8 teaspoon salt
1/8 teaspoon cream of tartar

Makes 8 servings
Each serving contains:
2 protein portions
146 calories
88 milligrams cholesterol

Combine milk and stock in a small saucepan and place over medium heat. In a large saucepan, melt the margarine and add the minced onion. Cook until onion is clear and tender. Add the flour and cook over medium heat, stirring constantly, 3 minutes, being careful not to brown flour. At this point, the milk and stock should be at the boiling point. Remove the saucepan containing the flour mixture from the heat and add the boiling milk and stock all at once, rapidly stirring with a wire whisk. Put this mixture back on medium heat and cook, stirring, until it has thickened. Remove from heat and add the 2 egg yolks, one at a time, stirring after each one is added. Add the salt, white pepper and Worcestershire sauce. You can stop at this point and continue the preparation of the soufflé just before it is to be served.

When you are ready to finish the soufflé, reheat the mixture to lukewarm and add the cheese and tuna, mixing thoroughly. Add the salt and cream of tartar to egg whites and beat stiff but not dry. Add one-third of the egg whites to the tuna mixture and stir in thoroughly to lighten the mixture. Carefully fold the remaining two-thirds of the beaten egg whites into the tuna, being careful not to overmix. Pour mixture into an 8-inch soufflé dish. Place in the center of a preheated 400° oven. Close door of the oven and immediately turn the temperature down to 375°. Cook soufflé 25 to 30 minutes and serve immediately.

MUSHROOM OMELET

liquid egg substitute = 2 eggs	Makes 1 serving which contains:	1/4 milk portion
1 teaspoon soy sauce	2 protein portions	222 calories
1/4 teaspoon corn oil	1 fat portion	2.5 milligrams cholesterol
1/4 cup Creamed Mushrooms, page 77		

Beat the egg substitute with the soy sauce until frothy. Heat the oil in an omelet pan (or a 10-inch cured iron skillet) until sizzling. Turn down the flame and pour in the beaten egg substitute. The egg mixture immediately starts to "set." Using a fork, scrape the "set" edges toward the center, tilting the pan at the same time so that the liquid seeps underneath to cook. When the bottom is cooked and the top is still a bit "runny," put in the Creamed Mushrooms in a thick line down the center third of the skillet. Fold the edges toward the center. Rest the edge of the pan on a plate and quickly turn the pan upside down so that the omelet slides out of the pan onto the plate.

eggs, egg substitutes and cheese

ANGELED EGGS

6 eggs
liquid egg substitute = 3 eggs
2 tablespoons safflower oil mayonnaise
1 tablespoon prepared mustard
1/4 teaspoon salt

1/8 teaspoon freshly ground
   black pepper
sugar substitute = 1/2 teaspoon sugar
2 teaspoons cider vinegar
paprika for garnish

Makes 12 portions
Each portion contains:
1/2 protein portion
37 calories
0 cholesterol

Hard boil the 6 eggs and cool to room temperature. Refrigerate until cold. Cook the liquid egg substitute as though you were making scrambled eggs. Mix the scrambled eggs thoroughly with all remaining ingredients, except hard-boiled eggs, using an electric blender, rotary hand beater or pastry blender. Cover and place mixture in refrigerater until cold. When the hard-boiled eggs have chilled, peel them and cut each egg in half lengthwise. Remove the yolks and place in a separate bowl to feed your pet (only if your veterinarian recommends cooked egg yolks for your pet). Fill each egg white half with the chilled egg substitute mixture, dividing the egg mixture evenly between them. Sprinkle top of filled egg whites with paprika for garnish. If you are storing the eggs, cover them before placing in the refrigerator.

Don't tell your friends these are not the usual deviled eggs and they will never know the difference! My Angeled Eggs are a variation of my friend, Helen Anne Bunn's deviled eggs. She is the friend most frequently asked to bring deviled eggs to picnics, so I felt her recipe would make the best basis for my variation.

fish

Fish is probably the best source of protein containing the least amount of fat. If you don't think you like fish, the chances are good you have never had it prepared properly, or that you never have had really *fresh* fish—or maybe both!

Taking first things first, find a good fish market or some source of fresh fish. If this is not possible, buy good fresh-frozen fish, thaw it in cold water, then prepare it immediately in the same manner described for fresh fish. I almost always prepare more fish than I plan to serve for the meal, because I love cold fish salad for luncheon the next day.

fish

BOUILLABAISSE

2 pounds fresh white fish (more than one kind of fish, if possible—bass, snapper, halibut, turbot, etc.)
2 lemons
salt
3 tablespoons corn oil
2 large onions, thinly sliced
1 leek, white part only, chopped
2 garlic buds, minced
3 large tomatoes, peeled, seeded and diced
2 tablespoons chopped parsley

1 stalk celery, finely chopped
1 bay leaf
1/4 teaspoon salt (1 teaspoon if using water instead of fish stock)
1/8 teaspoon fennel
1/8 teaspoon thyme
1/8 teaspoon saffron
dash of freshly ground black pepper
4 cups fish stock or water (fish stock makes a better bouillabaisse)
2 cups dry white wine (I like Chablis)
8 slices French bread

Makes 8 servings
Each serving contains:
3 protein portions
1 fat portion
1/2 B vegetable portion
282 calories without the bread
54 milligrams cholesterol

With the bread, add:
1 starch portion
68 calories
0 cholesterol

Wash the fish in cold water and pat dry. Place it in a glass baking dish and squeeze lemon juice on the fish. Lightly salt both sides. Cover the dish tightly with aluminum foil or lid, and place in the refrigerator until you plan to cook it.

In a deep kettle or Dutch oven, heat the corn oil. Add the onions and leeks and cook for 5 minutes. Add the garlic, tomatoes, parsley, celery, bay leaf, salt, fennel, thyme, saffron and pepper. Mix thoroughly and cook for 5 more minutes. Then, arrange the fish on top of the vegetables. Pour the stock (or water) and dry white wine over the fish. Cover and bring to a boil. Cook for about 8 to 10 minutes, or until fish has turned white.

The classic way to serve bouillabaisse is to remove the fish from the broth and arrange it on a serving platter. Each guest is then served a bowl of the broth poured over a slice of French bread. The fish is passed around and each person helps himself to the fish, putting it in his bowl of broth. I serve my bouillabaisse differently. I divide the fish equally in 8 bowls. Then, I spoon the broth over each serving and pass the bread. *And,* the fish is hot when served this way.

Marseilles, on the southern coast of France, is the undisputed bouillabaisse capital of the world. However, there is a great difference of opinion as to exactly what ingredients are essential to make it "authentic." Around Marseilles, you won't often find shellfish in bouillabaisse. Since shellfish has more cholesterol than fish, I decided to take the "Marseilles approach" in my own recipe.

SUNNY SEED SNAPPER

2 pounds red snapper (or filleted fish
   of your choice)
2 lemons
salt
3 tomatoes

1/4 teaspoon salt
2 tablespoons sunflower seeds
1 cup (1/4 pound) grated Monterey
   Jack cheese

Makes 8 servings

Each serving contains:
3 protein portions
1/2 fat portion
242 calories
63 milligrams cholesterol

If possible, always buy fresh fish. When it is necessary to use frozen fish, allow it to thaw completely before preparation. Wash fish in cold water and pat dry. Place in a flat glass baking dish and squeeze juice of 1 lemon on the fish and lightly salt it. Turn the fish over and squeeze juice of remaining lemon on it and again lightly salt it. Cover the dish tightly with aluminum foil or lid and place in the refrigerator until 30 minutes before you plan to cook it. When you are ready to cook the fish, remove from the refrigerator, allowing enough time for the dish to come to room temperature so that it will not break in the oven.

Dip each tomato in boiling water to remove skin. Peel and quarter the tomatoes, and steam in a steamer above boiling water until they are fork tender, about 3 to 5 minutes, depending on ripeness of the tomatoes. Put the steamed tomatoes in a bowl and add the salt. Mash the tomatoes with a fork, mixing thoroughly with the salt. Place the sunflower seeds in a 350° oven for 15 minutes, or until a golden brown in color. Grate the cheese and set aside with the tomatoes and sunflower seeds until the fish is cooked.

Cut the fish into 8 equal servings. Again tightly cover the baking dish containing the fish with aluminum foil and bake in a 350° oven for 20 to 30 minutes, or until fish is white all the way through. Remove the dish from the oven and pour off the excess liquid. Divide the mashed tomatoes evenly on top of fish; then sprinkle the sunflower seeds evenly over the mashed tomatoes. Divide the grated cheese evenly over the entire dish. Put the fish under the broiler for approximately 1 minute, or until cheese is completely melted. Place on individual plates or serving platter.

fish

BASS À LA PAUL BOCUSE
(Sort Of)

1 6- to 7-pound striped bass
2 lemons
salt
2 tablespoons fresh tarragon, or
1 tablespoon dry tarragon

6 bay leaves
salt and white pepper
2 cups (1 recipe) French Herb
   Sauce, page 40
fresh tarragon or parsley for garnish

Makes 12 servings
Each serving contains:
3 protein portions
219 calories
70 milligrams cholesterol

If possible, always buy fresh fish. When it is necessary to use frozen fish, allow it to thaw completely before preparation. Clean, skin and debone bass. Leave the head on for picturesque presentation. (If a whole fish is unavailable, use filleted bass; it tastes just as good but is not so tremendous looking.)

Wash fish in cold water and pat dry. Place in a flat glass baking dish and squeeze juice of 1 lemon on the fish and lightly salt. Turn the fish over and squeeze juice of remaining lemon on it and again lightly salt. Cover the dish tightly with aluminum foil or lid and place in the refrigerator until 30 minutes before you plan to cook it.

When you are ready to cook the fish, remove from the refrigerator, allowing enough time for the dish to come to room temperature so that it will not break in the oven. Sprinkle both sides of the fish with salt and pepper. Stuff the fish with tarragon and bay leaves. Wrap fish in aluminum foil and bake at 350° for 40 minutes. Remove foil and place fish on a serving platter. Pour French Herb Sauce over top, totally covering the fish. Garnish with fresh tarragon or parsley.

Paul Bocuse is one of the greatest of the famous French chefs in Lyons. This dish I named for him, happily remembering the beautiful afternoon I ordered bass in his restaurant.

CURRIED FISH CASSEROLE

3 tablespoons corn oil margarine
3 medium-size onions, coarsely
  chopped
5 tablespoons flour
1 tablespoon curry powder
1/4 teaspoon ground ginger
1-1/2 teaspoons salt

dash of white pepper
1 cup chicken stock
2 cups low-fat milk, at boiling point
2 pounds cooked fish, cubed (a marvelous way to use leftover fish!)
1 teaspoon freshly squeezed lemon juice
4 cups cooked white rice

Makes 12 servings
Each serving contains:
2 protein portions
3/4 fat portion
1 starch portion
247 calories
52 milligrams cholesterol

Melt the margarine in a large heavy iron skillet. Add the chopped onion and cook until onion is clear and tender. Combine the flour, curry powder, ginger, salt and white pepper and add to onion to make a paste, cooking about 3 minutes. Heat chicken stock until hot and add to flour mixture, cooking again for another 3 minutes to form a thick paste. Remove from heat and add the milk (which is at boiling point) to the onion mixture *all at once,* stirring with a wire whisk. Return to heat and simmer, stirring occasionally until thickened, about 10 minutes. Add the cubed, cooked fish and lemon juice to the sauce and mix thoroughly. Add the cooked rice and fold in thoroughly. Pour the entire mixture in a large, ovenproof casserole and bake at 325° for 1 hour and 15 minutes, or until thoroughly heated.

I always make this dish the day before I plan to serve it, cover it tightly and refrigerate overnight. I then remove it from the refrigerator to allow it to come to room temperature before cooking it. I think the flavor is better when prepared ahead of time.

fish

PARTY FISH PLATTER

2 pounds firm, fresh fish (halibut or bass is excellent)
1 cup coarsely chopped celery
1 cup coarsely chopped onions
1 carrot, sliced
1 bunch fresh parsley, chopped stems and leaves
2 cups dry white wine (I like Chablis)
1/2 teaspoon salt

dash of white pepper
1 envelope unflavored gelatin
3 tablespoons water
1 bay leaf
1/2 cup safflower oil mayonnaise
1/2 cup minced parsley
optional for garnish:
fresh tarragon
pimiento

capers
or use your imagination!

Makes 8 servings
Each serving contains:
3 protein portions
3 fat portions
354 calories
54 milligrams cholesterol

If possible, always buy fresh fish. When it is necessary to use frozen fish, allow to thaw completely before preparation. Put the fish in a large saucepan. Add the celery, onion, carrot and chopped parsley. Mix the salt and pepper with the wine and pour over all of the ingredients in the saucepan. If the wine does not cover completely, add a little more wine. Bring to a simmer and cover. Cook 8 to 10 minutes or until fish turns white. Remove from heat and allow to come to room temperature. Remove fish from poaching liquid and arrange on a serving platter, reserving liquid. Cover the platter tightly with aluminum foil or saran wrap and place in refrigerator.

Soften the gelatin in the 3 tablespoons water. Put the poaching liquid back on the heat and bring to a boil. Strain the hot liquid, reserving 1-3/4 cups. Add the softened gelatin to the hot 1-3/4 cups of liquid and mix until gelatin is thoroughly dissolved. Add the bay leaf and allow the mixture to come to room temperature; then cover it and place in the refrigerator for about 1 hour or until it is slightly jelled. At this point, remove the bay leaf and add the safflower mayonnaise to the gelatin mixture. Using a wire whisk, mix thoroughly.

Remove the cold platter of fish from the refrigerator. Spoon the gelatin-mayonnaise mixture evenly over the entire fish platter. Sprinkle the minced parsley evenly over the top. Re-cover the platter of fish and put back in the refrigerator until firmly jelled. Garnish as desired. This makes a lovely luncheon or summer supper dish. I like to serve this with Cucumbers Dilly Dilly and hot Indian Curry Bread.

fish

DILLIED FISH AMANDINE

2 pounds solid white fish (red
   snapper is my favorite)
2 lemons
salt
2 teaspoons tarragon

1 cup Sauce Dilly Dilly, page 44
Toasted Almond Flakes (using 14
   almonds), page 45

Makes 8 servings

Each serving contains:
3 protein portions
2-1/4 fat portions
320 calories
60 milligrams cholesterol

If possible, always buy fresh fish. When it is necessary to use frozen fish, allow it to thaw completely before preparation. Wash fish in cold water and pat dry. Place in a flat glass baking dish, squeeze juice of 1 lemon on the fish and lightly salt it. Turn the fish over and squeeze juice of remaining lemon on it and again lightly salt. Cover the dish tightly with aluminum foil or lid and place in the refrigerator until 30 minutes before you plan to cook it.

When you are ready to cook the fish, remove from the refrigerator, allowing enough time for the dish to come to room temperature so that it will not break in the oven. Crush the tarragon, using a mortar and pestle, and sprinkle it lightly and evenly over the fish. Again, tightly cover the baking dish with aluminum foil and place in a 350° oven for 15 minutes (a little longer if the fish is extremely thick). Remove the dish from the oven and pour off all excess liquid. Spoon Sauce Dilly Dilly evenly over the fish. Place under the broiler until sauce starts to bubble (this only takes a minute). Remove the fish from under the broiler and carefully place each piece of fish on the serving platter or individual plates as you desire. Evenly sprinkle the almond flakes on top of each serving. This is my favorite "fish dish."

TAHITIAN TERIYAKI SWORDFISH STEAKS

2 pounds firm swordfish steaks
1 cup Tahitian Teriyaki Marinade,
    following

Makes 8 servings
Each serving contains:

3 protein portions
219 calories
36 milligrams cholesterol

Marinate the fish steaks in the marinade in the refrigerator for 3 hours before cooking. Broil the steaks approximately 5 minutes per side (depending on the thickness of the steaks), basting frequently with the marinade so that the fish does not become dry.

TAHITIAN TERIYAKI MARINADE

1 tablespoon sesame seeds
1/2 cup beef or chicken stock
1/4 cup unsweetened pineapple juice
1/4 cup Sherry

2 tablespoons soy sauce
1 tablespoon Champagne vinegar
sugar substitute = 1 teaspoon sugar
1 garlic bud, crushed

Makes 1 cup
Free food, calories negligible
0 cholesterol

This is an excellent marinade for fish as well as meat or chicken, and is especially good when the meat is charcoal broiled. When using the marinade for beef, use beef stock; when using it for chicken or seafood, use chicken stock.

Place sesame seeds in a 350° oven for 15 minutes, or until they are a golden brown in color. Put all ingredients in a blender and blend until sesame seeds are pulverized. Allow the fish or meats to marinate for 2 or 3 hours and then serve the marinade, warmed, in a gravy boat to be used on the fish or meat as a sauce.

fish

FISH FILLETS FLORENTINE

2 pounds fresh white fish (I like sea
    bass or red snapper)
2 lemons
salt
1 pound fresh spinach, chopped, or
2 9-ounce packages of frozen
    chopped spinach

1-1/2 cups Basic White Sauce, page 38
1/2 cup grated low-fat Mozzarella
    cheese
1/8 teaspoon ground nutmeg
1/8 teaspoon white pepper
1 tablespoon grated Parmesan cheese

Each serving contains:
3-1/4 protein portions
1/4 fat portion
1/4 milk portion
280 calories
67.4 milligrams cholesterol

Makes 8 servings

If possible, always buy fresh fish. When it is necessary to use frozen fish, allow it to thaw completely before preparation. Wash the fish in cold water and pat dry. Place in a flat glass baking dish and squeeze juice of 1 lemon on the fish and lightly salt. Turn the fish over and squeeze juice of remaining lemon on it and again lightly salt. Cover the dish tightly with aluminum foil or lid and place in the refrigerator.

When you are ready to cook the fish, remove from the refrigerator, allowing enough time for the dish to come to room temperature so that it will not break in the oven. Place the covered dish in a 350° oven for about 20 minutes or until the fillets turn white.

While the fish is cooking, cook the spinach and drain it using a colander or a strainer. Press the spinach with the back of a spoon to extract all the liquid. Line the bottom of another 8x12 glass baking dish with the spinach. Place the cooked fish on top of the spinach and pour the juices from the fish over the top of the entire dish.

Combine the white sauce, Mozzarella cheese, nutmeg and white pepper in a saucepan and beat until the cheese is completely melted. Pour the cheese mixture evenly over the top of the fish. Sprinkle the Parmesan cheese evenly over the top of the entire dish. Put the dish back in a 350° oven for 10 more minutes and then place it under the broiler until the top is lightly browned.

FILLET-OF-SOLE IN ORANGE SAUCE

8 small fillets (2 pounds)
2 lemons
salt
paprika
1 tablespoon cornstarch
1/2 cup freshly squeezed orange juice

1/4 teaspoon salt
1/4 teaspoon ground cinnamon
1/4 teaspoon peeled and grated
   ginger root, or
1/8 teaspoon powdered ginger
2 teaspoons freshly grated orange peel
1 orange, peeled and thinly sliced
   (use orange you just grated!)

Makes 8 servings
Each serving contains:
3 protein portions
1/4 fruit portion
229 calories
54 milligrams cholesterol

If possible, always buy fresh fish. When it is necessary to use frozen fish, allow it to thaw completely before preparation. Wash fish in cold water and pat dry. Place in a flat glass baking dish and squeeze juice of 1 lemon on the fish; lightly salt it and sprinkle with paprika. Turn the fish over and squeeze juice of remaining lemon on it; again lightly salt and sprinkle with paprika. Cover the dish tightly with aluminum foil or lid and place in the refrigerator until 30 minutes before you plan to cook it. When you are ready to cook the fish, remove from the refrigerator, allowing enough time for the dish to come to room temperature so that it will not break in the oven.

In a saucepan, dissolve the cornstarch in the orange juice. Add the salt, cinnamon and ginger. Grate the orange peel, being careful to use only the peel as the white section of the orange tends to be bitter. Add the grated orange peel to the cornstarch mixture in the saucepan and cook over low heat, stirring constantly, until slightly thickened. Pour the orange sauce over the fish in the glass baking dish. Cover tightly with aluminum foil and place in a 350° oven for 10 to 12 minutes, or until the sole has turned white and is easily flaked with a fork. Remove the sole and place on a serving platter or individual plates. Spoon the orange sauce over the top of the sole and cover each piece with orange slices. I like to serve this with Pine Nut Pilaf with raisins and a steamed green vegetable.

fish

SCANDINAVIAN PICKLED SALMON

1 teaspoon dried dill weed
1 teaspoon dill seeds
2 tablespoons salt
sugar substitute = 2 teaspoons sugar

1/4 teaspoon freshly ground black
  pepper
2 pounds fresh salmon (a center section
  fillet with the skin is best!)
3/4 cup red wine vinegar

Each 1 ounce or 2 2x3-inch thin slices
  salmon contain:
1 protein portion
73 calories
18.4 milligrams cholesterol

Using a mortar and pestle, crush the dill weed, dill seed, salt, sugar substitute and pepper together thoroughly. Sprinkle half of this mixture in the bottom of a glass dish just large enough to hold the salmon. Place the salmon, skin side down, in the dish and rub the remaining herb mixture into the fish well, using your hands. Pour the vinegar over the fish and cover tightly with saran wrap or aluminum foil. Place a weight of at least 1 pound on top of the fish (I use a can of fruit or vegetables for this purpose!). Refrigerate for at least 2 days, spooning the juices over the marinating salmon as frequently as possible (at least 5 times a day).

Slice thinly to serve as hors d'oeuvre, appetizer, or if you like this as much as I do, you might want to use it for your main course. When serving this dish as a main course, I like a large tossed green salad and cold, thinly sliced potatoes with just a few capers sprinkled on them as accompaniments. I always top the salmon with Cooked Mustard Sauce.

SOCKEYE SALMON MOUSSE

2 cups sockeye salmon (1 16-ounce
   can or 2 7-3/4-ounce cans)
1 cup low-fat Jelled Milk, page 39
2/3 cup chicken stock, cold
1/8 teaspoon white pepper

1/4 teaspoon salt
1 teaspoon Worcestershire sauce
2 tablespoons freshly squeezed
   lemon juice
2 tablespoons grated onion

Each serving contains:
2 protein portions
1/4 milk portion
177 calories
51.9 milligrams cholesterol

Makes 4 servings

Open the canned salmon and drain thoroughly. Put the drained salmon in a mixing bowl and mash well with a fork, breaking up the salmon into *very small* pieces. Combine all ingredients except the salmon and blend until smooth. Slowly add the mashed salmon a little at a time until all of the salmon has been blended and the mixture is again smooth. Pour the smooth salmon mixture into an oiled 4-cup mold. (I like to use a fish-shaped mold.) The mixture will fill a 4-cup mold to the very top, so you must be very careful not to spill any of it when covering and placing it in the refrigerator. To unmold, tap the bottom of the mold and place a plate over the top; invert quickly in an even movement on to a platter. If the mousse does not unmold, dip it in warm water for a few seconds and try again.

This makes an unusually pretty luncheon dish when done in a fish mold. You can then decorate the fish with capers and pimiento and place parsley or fresh dill around the fish on the platter. I like to serve this with marinated cold vegetables, sliced tomatoes and hot Herb Bread.

poultry

Chicken and the white meat of turkey closely follow fish as a desirable source of protein for a happy heart. Chicken is fun to cook because it offers infinite variety in taste range. It is much more difficult to think of a way you can't cook chicken than to dream up a new and unusual recipe. Many of my recipes specifically call for boned chicken breasts. I like to use the boned breasts for several reasons: They are low in fat, easiest to eat, and make the most attractive presentation. If possible, when preparing chicken breasts, have your butcher bone, skin and halve them for you. If *you* are boning them yourself, remove the bone from the entire breast and then remove the skin before cutting the breasts in half. It is easier to bone whole chicken breasts than the half breast.

BAKED CHICKEN BREASTS

4 whole chicken breasts
2 tablespoons freshly squeezed
    lemon juice
salt and white pepper
4 teaspoons corn oil margarine

1/4 cup dry white wine (I use Chablis)
1/2 cup chicken stock

Makes 8 servings

Each serving contains approximately:
2 protein portions
1/2 fat portion
169 calories
44.8 milligrams cholesterol

Bone, skin and then halve the chicken breasts; remove all visible fat. Place chicken in flat baking dish just large enough to hold the 8 breast halves. *Do not overlap.* Sprinkle evenly with lemon juice and lightly sprinkle each breast with salt and white pepper. Put 1/2 teaspoon of corn oil margarine over each breast, rubbing it into the surface with the back of a spoon. Then combine the wine and stock and pour over all.

Cover baking dish tightly with aluminum foil and place in 400° oven for about 25 to 30 minutes. At this point, check to see if the chicken is properly cooked. It should be completely white and spring back to the touch when pressed with your finger. If the chicken is not completely done, re-cover tightly and place back in the oven for a few more minutes. Be careful not to overcook the chicken as it then becomes dry and loses its flavor.

poultry

CHICKEN BREASTS VERONIQUE

4 whole chicken breasts
salt and white pepper
2 tablespoons freshly squeezed
   lemon juice
4 teaspoons corn oil
3/4 cup white wine (I prefer Chablis)

2 cups seedless grapes (80 grapes)
3 tablespoons cornstarch
3 tablespoons cold water
3/4 cup Basic White Sauce, page 38

Makes 8 servings

Each serving contains:
2 protein portions
3/4 fat portion
1/4 fruit portion
1/4 starch portion
208 calories
46.7 milligrams cholesterol

Bone, skin and then halve the chicken breasts; remove all visible fat. Place the boned breasts in a flat baking dish just large enough to hold the 8 pieces of chicken. *Do not overlap.* Sprinkle lightly with salt and white pepper. Turn and sprinkle again with salt and white pepper. Sprinkle evenly with lemon juice. Pour 1/2 teaspoon corn oil over each breast, rubbing into the surface with back of spoon. Pour wine over the chicken. Add the grapes, distributing evenly over chicken.

Cover baking dish tightly with aluminum foil and place in a 400° oven for 30 minutes. At this point check to see if the chicken is properly cooked. It should be completely white and spring back to the touch when pressed with your finger. If it is not completely done, re-cover tightly and replace in the oven for a few minutes. Be careful *not to overcook* the chicken because it can become dry and lose much of its flavor.

When chicken is cooked, remove foil cover and place chicken breasts and grapes either on individual plates or a serving platter and cover to keep warm. Pour the liquid in which the chicken was cooked into a saucepan. Mix the cornstarch and water until smooth and add to the cooking liquid; bring mixture to a boil. Simmer, stirring constantly until thickened. Add the Basic White Sauce to the mixture and mix thoroughly. Pour the sauce over the chicken breasts.

HAWAIIAN CHICKEN

3 tablespoons sesame seeds
4 whole chicken breasts
salt and white pepper
2 tablespoons freshly squeezed
  lemon juice
4 teaspoons corn oil
2 cups diced unsweetened fresh
  or canned pineapple

1/4 cup Champagne vinegar
1/4 cup Sherry
2 tablespoons soy sauce
sugar substitute = 2 teaspoons sugar

Makes 8 servings

Each serving contains:
2 protein portions
1/2 fruit portion
1 fat portion
211 calories
44.8 milligrams cholesterol

Place sesame seeds in a 350° oven for 15 minutes, or until a golden brown in color. Bone, skin and then halve chicken breasts; remove all visible fat. Place the chicken breasts in a flat baking dish just large enough to hold the 8 pieces of chicken. *Do not overlap.* Sprinkle lightly with salt and white pepper. Turn and sprinkle again with salt and white pepper. Sprinkle evenly with lemon juice. Pour 1/2 teaspoon corn oil over each breast, rubbing it into the surface with the back of a spoon. Cover the chicken evenly with the diced pineapple.

Place all other ingredients in the blender and blend until the toasted sesame seeds are completely pulverized. Pour the blended sauce evenly over the chicken and pineapple in the baking dish and cover tightly with a lid or aluminum foil. Place in a 400° oven for 40 minutes. When the chicken is cooked, remove the foil and serve the chicken breasts, spooning the sauce and pineapple equally over each serving. This dish is excellent served with Pine Nut Pilaf.

poultry

PARTY CHICKEN PLATTER

6 whole chicken breasts
1 cup coarsely chopped celery
1 cup coarsely chopped onion
1 carrot, sliced
1 bunch fresh parsley, stems and
   leaves chopped
2 cups dry white wine (I like Chablis)
1 teaspoon salt

dash of white pepper
1 envelope unflavored gelatin
3 tablespoons water
1 bay leaf
1/2 cup safflower oil mayonnaise
1/2 cup finely minced parsley
optional for garnish:
cucumber slices, carrot curls,
pimiento, radish roses, etc.

Makes 12 servings
Each serving contains:
2 protein portions
2 fat portions
236 calories
50 milligrams cholesterol

Bone, skin and then halve chicken breasts; remove all visible fat. Put the chicken breasts in a large saucepan and add the celery, onion, carrot and parsley to the chicken. Mix the salt and pepper with the wine and pour over the chicken and vegetables. If the wine does not cover completely, add a little more wine. Bring to a simmer and cover, simmering 30 to 40 minutes, or until chicken breasts are done. Remove from heat and allow to cool to room temperature. Remove chicken breasts from the pan and arrange them on a large platter, reserving liquid. Cover the chicken breasts tightly with aluminum foil or saran wrap. Place in the refrigerator.

Put the poaching liquid back on the heat and bring to a boil. Soften the gelatin in the water. Strain the poaching liquid and reserve 1-3/4 cups. Add the softened gelatin to the reserved liquid and mix until all gelatin is thoroughly dissolved. Add the bay leaf and allow the mixture to come to room temperature. After it has reached room temperature, place it in the refrigerator for about 1 hour, or until it is slightly jelled. At this point, remove the bay leaf and add the safflower mayonnaise to the gelatin mixture. Using a wire whisk, mix thoroughly.

Remove the cold platter of chicken breasts from the refrigerator and spoon the gelatin-mayonnaise mixture over each breast, covering entire platter. Sprinkle the minced parsley evenly over top of chicken breasts. Re-cover and put platter back in the refrigerator until firmly jelled. This makes a beautiful luncheon or light supper dish. Garnish as you wish with my suggested garnish or with your own favorites.

COQ AU VIN

4 whole chicken breasts
3 tablespoons corn oil margarine
1 garlic bud, minced
salt and freshly ground black pepper
12 small boiling onions, peeled

12 large fresh mushrooms
2 cups Brown Sauce, page 37

Makes 8 servings

Each serving contains:
2 protein portions
1 fat portion
1 B vegetable portion
227 calories
44.8 milligrams cholesterol

Bone, skin and then halve the chicken breasts; remove all visible fat. Melt margarine in a large cured iron skillet. Add the garlic and cook a few minutes. Salt and pepper both sides of the chicken breasts. Put chicken in skillet and cook until a rich deep brown on one side.

While the chicken is browning, put the onions in a large saucepan with lightly salted water and cook, covered, about 12 minutes, or until fork tender. Carefully wash the mushrooms and remove the stems. When the chicken is browned on one side, add the mushroom caps and cook with the chicken until the other side is also brown. Put the chicken and mushrooms in a flat baking dish. Drain the onions and add them to the chicken. Pour Brown Sauce over the entire dish. Place, uncovered, in a 350° oven for 30 minutes. I often make this dish in the morning up to the point where it goes in the oven. Then, I put it in the refrigerator until dinner time. Take it out at least 1 hour before you plan to put it in the oven. I think the flavor is even better if it is made ahead, as I have suggested.

I like to serve Coq au Vin with rice pilaf and a steamed fresh green vegetable, such as peas or asparagus.

poultry

LEMON CHICKEN IN ENVELOPES

4 whole chicken breasts
salt
2 teaspoons minced fresh tarragon, or
1 teaspoon dry tarragon

4 lemons, cut in half
steamed broccoli or
any fresh, green group A vegetable

Makes 8 servings

Each serving contains:
2 protein portions
146 calories
44.8 milligrams cholesterol

Bone, skin and then halve the chicken breasts; remove all visible fat. Place each halved breast on a 12-inch-square piece of aluminum foil and lightly salt both sides of the chicken. Sprinkle each breast evenly with 1/4 teaspoon tarragon. Fold the aluminum foil in half, leaving the breast in the center. Then fold each end over twice (about 1 inch for each fold), so that it is possible to squeeze the lemon juice on to the chicken without its running out of the foil envelope. Into each envelope squeeze the juice of a 1/2 lemon. Then, holding the envelope upright, fold the top side of the envelope over twice, pressing to seal after each fold. Place all 8 envelopes in a flat baking dish and bake in a 400° oven for approximately 20 minutes.

Remove dish from the oven. Unfold top of envelope and pour the juice over the steamed vegetables. Broccoli just happens to be my favorite with this particular sauce, but you may use any group A vegetable of your choice. Remove the chicken from the envelope and place beside vegetable on serving platter or individual plates and serve immediately. This is a delightfully different, very low-calorie meal!

poultry

FLAMING GAME HENS

3 Cornish game hens, halved
salt and white pepper
2 tablespoons imitation bacon bits
1-1/2 cups seedless grapes
1 tablespoon corn oil margarine

2 green onions, including green tops,
    finely chopped
1/2 cup Port
3/4 cup Basic White Sauce, page 38
1/2 cup flaming Brandy, warmed

Makes 8 servings

Each serving contains:
2 protein portions
3/4 fat portion
1/4 fruit portion
190 calories
46.7 milligrams cholesterol

Sprinkle both sides of game hens with salt and pepper. Place split game hens cut side down in a flat baking dish in which they fit closely. Sprinkle the bacon bits evenly over the top of the hens. Place pan in a 350° oven for 50 minutes.

While game hens are baking, put the grapes in a saucepan of boiling water, cover and simmer for 5 minutes. Melt the margarine in another saucepan. Add the finely chopped green onions and sauté for 3 minutes. Drain the grapes and add to the onions. Add the Port wine. When it starts to simmer, ignite the wine and stir until the flame goes out. Slowly add the Basic White Sauce, stirring constantly.

Remove the game hens from the oven and place on a metal serving tray. Put the game hens on the table or a serving cart. Pour the warmed brandy over the game hens and ignite. Serve flaming.

Do not flame the game hens in the kitchen and then carry them to the table. This can be dangerous!

TURKEY PROVENCAL

8 thin slices turkey breast, without skin
salt and freshly ground black pepper
2 teaspoons corn oil margarine
3 garlic buds, minced
4 ripe tomatoes, peeled and quartered

8 small carrots, sliced and parboiled
    until fork tender
2 cups Brown Sauce, page 37

Makes 8 servings

Each serving contains:
2 protein portions
1 B vegetable portion
1/4 fat portion
193 calories
44.8 milligrams cholesterol

Place the slices of turkey breast in a baking dish and lightly salt and pepper both sides. In a saucepan melt the margarine and add the garlic. Cook 5 minutes. Add the tomatoes and carrots. Cook until the tomatoes are soft. Add the Brown Sauce and mix well. Pour sauce over turkey slices. Bake, uncovered, in a 350° oven for 30 minutes.

This is a delightfully different way to use leftover holiday turkey. Serve with unbuttered crusty French bread and a crisp green salad with Happy Heart Dressing.

meat

Red meats contain greater amounts of animal fat than either fish or chicken. Beef, lamb and pork are usually restricted to three meals per week. Veal is almost in a category by itself, because it is lower in fat than other meats. For this reason it is usually allowed more frequently.

Always buy the leanest cut of meat available. Then, before cooking the meat, carefully remove any excess fat. When purchasing ground meat, ask your butcher to remove *all* fat before grinding it. This may seem extravagant when you pay for it, but you will have so much less shrinkage when cooking it that you will not really be losing money.

When broiling meat, use a slotted broiling pan or a charcoal barbecue so that the fat can drip off the meat during the cooking. When preparing any boiled meat, such as stew, chill overnight and skim off all fat which forms on the top before reheating and serving. When making gravies from your roasts, always use Defatted Drippings, page 35.

Meat substitutes are still another category in the meat recipe section. Recently, many new brands have come on the market. Many are excellent in appearance, texture and flavor.

meat

PRETEND PÂTÉ

1 envelope unflavored gelatin
1-1/2 cups beef stock
1 8-ounce package ham substitute
   slices

1 teaspoon grated onion
1 teaspoon freshly squeezed lemon
   juice

Makes 10 servings

Each serving contains:
1/2 protein portion
36 calories
0 cholesterol

Soften gelatin in the cold beef stock for at least 5 minutes. Stir over low heat until completely dissolved. *Do not boil.* Pour 1/4 cup of the beef stock into an oiled 2-cup mold and chill until firm (this takes a very short time!).

Cook ham slices in a cured heavy iron skillet until they are lightly browned on both sides. Then, place slices in the blender one at a time with the remaining consommé and blend until smooth. Pour the mixture into a mixing bowl and add the grated onion and lemon juice, mixing thoroughly. Pour the entire mixture onto the mold on top of the thin, jelled layer of consommé. Chill until firm.

To unmold, tap the bottom of the mold and place a plate over the top. Invert *quickly* in an even movement to unmold the pâté on the serving plate. This is an excellent hors d'oeuvre or first course. It also makes a fabulous sandwich spread.

SPAGHETTI SAUCE, BOLOGNESE STYLE

1-1/2 teaspoons corn oil
1 tablespoon imitation bacon bits
1 medium-size carrot, scraped and
   grated
1 medium-size onion, minced
1 stalk celery, minced
1/2 green bell pepper, seeded
   and minced
1 pound lean ground veal
1/4 cup tomato sauce

1/2 cup dry white wine (I like Chablis)
1/2 teaspoon salt
1/4 teaspoon freshly ground black
   pepper
1/8 teaspoon ground nutmeg
1 cup beef stock
1-1/2 teaspoons corn oil margarine
1 cup (1/4 pound) sliced fresh mushrooms
1/2 cup low-fat milk, warmed

Makes 6 servings
Each serving of sauce contains:
2-1/2 protein portions
1/2 fat portion
206 calories
77 milligrams cholesterol
Each 1/2 cup of cooked noodles
   contains:
1 starch portion
68 calories
0 cholesterol

Heat the oil in a cured iron skillet. Add the bacon bits, carrot, onion, celery and green pepper. When vegetables are lightly browned, add ground veal. Stir frequently so veal will brown evenly. Add tomato sauce, white wine, salt, pepper, nutmeg and beef stock. Cover and simmer for 20 minutes. While meat is simmering, place the 1-1/2 teaspoons margarine in another skillet and sauté the mushrooms until tender. Then add the mushrooms and milk to the sauce; mix and heat thoroughly. Serve over noodles.

meat

STEAK TARTARE

1-1/2 pounds freshly ground sirloin, ground once
2 tablespoons freshly squeezed lemon juice
3/4 teaspoon salt
1/4 teaspoon freshly ground black pepper
2 tablespoons Worcestershire sauce
2 drops Tabasco sauce
1 teaspoon Dijon-style mustard

1/4 cup capers
1/4 cup minced onion
1/4 cup minced parsley
1/2 pint imitation sour cream
4 additional teaspoons Dijon-style mustard
For Garnish:
1/4 cup capers
1/4 cup minced onion
1/2 cup minced parsley
1 large tomato, peeled and finely diced

1/4 cup finely diced green bell pepper
freshly ground black pepper to taste

Makes 8 servings as an entrée
Each serving contains:
3 protein portions
3 fat portions
354 calories
90.9 milligrams cholesterol

Have your butcher remove all fat from the sirloin and grind it *once.* Always try to have the meat ground the day you are going to use it.

Put the meat in a large mixing bowl. In another bowl mix the lemon juice and salt until the salt is dissolved. Add the pepper, Worcestershire sauce, Tabasco and 1 teaspoon mustard, mixing thoroughly. Add to the meat and again mix thoroughly. Then add capers, onion and parsley and mix thoroughly. Divide meat into 2 equal parts, making large patties out of each half, 8 inches in diameter.

Mix the imitation sour cream with the 4 teaspoons mustard thoroughly, using a wire whisk. Place the first meat patty on a serving platter and frost just as you would frost a cake with half of the sour cream and mustard mixture. Sprinkle the top of this patty, using half of each of the garnish ingredients: capers, onion, parsley, tomato and green pepper. Sprinkle with freshly ground pepper and then place the second meat patty on top as you would the second layer of a cake. Frost both patties with the remaining sour cream and mustard mixture. Sprinkle remaining garnish ingredients over the top in a decorative manner. At this point your Steak Tartare should look like a gorgeous vegetable cake. Cover and refrigerate before serving.

To serve for hors d'oeuvre, place serving knife around the edge of the meat cake and have a plate of thinly sliced pumpernickel, rye or French bread next to it. Melba toast is good, too. I also serve this as an entrée for 8 people, bringing it to the table on the serving platter and then serving it on 8 individual plates and passing the bread.

I call this recipe Mona's Steak Tartare Cake! That's because Mona Freeman Ellis taught me how to make it. Actually, it is *my* version of Mona's version of Peter Canlis' Steak Tartare! All of them are delicious. However, mine is the lowest in cholesterol.

THE DRINKING MAN'S POT ROAST

1 teaspoon corn oil
3 pounds lean pot roast (your favorite cut)
flour
salt
1/2 cup Burgundy
1 cup Sherry
3 cups beef stock
1/4 teaspoon sweet basil
1/4 teaspoon marjoram

1/4 teaspoon thyme
2 bay leaves, broken
4 carrots, scraped and halved
4 small potatoes, peeled and halved
3 onions, quartered
1 tablespoon corn oil margarine
2 cups sliced fresh mushrooms
2 shallots, chopped
6 tablespoons Madeira

Makes 8 servings
Each serving contains:
3 protein portions
1 B vegetable portion
1/2 starch portion
1/2 fat portion
312 calories
94 milligrams cholesterol

Put 1 teaspoon oil in a cured heavy iron skillet and heat. Flour and salt completely the pot roast. Brown roast over medium heat, turning frequently, for 1 hour. Add Burgundy and simmer off until dry; then add 1/2 cup Sherry and simmer off. Add remaining 1/2 cup of Sherry and simmer off.

Combine the beef stock with all of the herbs and pour over pot roast. Cover and cook approximately 1-1/2 hours. Add carrots, potatoes and onions and cook approximately 30 minutes. While the vegetables are cooking, sauté the mushrooms and shallots in 1 tablespoon margarine. When the other vegetables are fork tender, add the mushrooms and shallots and 3 tablespoons of Madeira to the pot roast and simmer together for 10 minutes. Add the remaining 3 tablespoons of Madeira, mix and serve.

ROAST BEEF HASH

2 cups finely chopped cooked roast
   beef
2 large raw potatoes, grated
2 cups finely chopped onion
1 garlic bud, minced
2 cups beef stock

1 teaspoon salt
1/4 teaspoon freshly ground black
   pepper
1 teaspoon Worcestershire sauce

Makes 4 servings

Each serving contains:
2 protein portions
1 starch portion
1 B vegetable portion
323 calories
60.6 milligrams cholesterol

Chop the roast beef, making sure there is *no fat* left on the part you are using. Put the roast beef, potatoes and onions in a flat baking dish and place it under the broiler until brown, stirring frequently to brown deeply and evenly. Put the browned meat and vegetables in a cured heavy iron skillet. Add all other ingredients and mix well. Simmer over medium heat until potatoes are tender and all liquid is absorbed. Pat surface down with the back of a large spoon, and again place under the broiler to brown and crisp the top.

If you wish to make this ahead of time to serve the following day, cool to room temperature after simmering, and put in a flat baking dish. Cover tightly and refrigerate until you are ready to serve the hash. Put it in a 350° oven for about 15 minutes to heat thoroughly and then put it under the broiler to brown and crisp prior to serving. I really think it tastes better when you hold it a day before serving.

meat

MINI MEAT LOAVES

1 teaspoon corn oil
4 large onions, peeled and thinly sliced
3 pounds lean ground round
2 teaspoons salt
1/4 teaspoon white pepper

3 cups unsweetened applesauce (make it just like Effie's Baked Applesauce, page 135, omitting sugar substitute)
6 slices whole-wheat bread, cut in 1/4-inch cubes

Makes 12 servings

Each serving contains:
1 B vegetable portion
3 protein portions
1/2 fruit portion
1/2 starch portion
285 calories
91 milligrams cholesterol

Put the teaspoon of corn oil in a cured heavy iron skillet over medium heat. Add the onions and cook, stirring frequently, 30 minutes. Reduce heat and continue cooking until onions are brown.

Place meat in a large mixing bowl and mix thoroughly with the salt and pepper. Add the applesauce and mix; then add the cubed bread and mix. Cover until the onions are ready. When cool enough to handle, add the onions to the meat and mix thoroughly. Divide mixture into 12 mini, ball-shaped meat loaves. Bake at 325° for 45 minutes in a shallow baking dish. Or, if you prefer, you can make 2 regular-size loaves and bake at 325° for 1 hour.

VEAL CUTLETS IN MUSHROOM SAUCE

2 pounds veal cutlets (8 small cutlets, not breaded)
3 tablespoons corn oil margarine
2 cups sliced fresh mushrooms
4 cups Brown Sauce, page 37

Makes 8 servings
Each serving contains:

3 protein portions
1 fat portion
1/4 starch portion
290 calories
87 milligrams cholesterol

In a large cured heavy iron skillet, brown the veal cutlets over medium heat. Continue cooking until cutlets are fork tender. While the veal cutlets are cooking, melt the margarine in another skillet and sauté the mushrooms until tender. Add the Brown Sauce to the mushrooms and heat thoroughly. Pour the mushroom sauce mixture over the veal cutlets and place on a serving platter or individual plates, spooning the brown mushroom sauce evenly over the top of the cutlets. This is so delicious! I serve it at least once a week in my home.

VEAL PARMIGIANO

1 pound veal steak, pounded thin
1 tablespoon corn oil
3 garlic buds, minced
1 medium-size onion, peeled and
    minced
2-1/2 cups chopped, peeled
    tomatoes or
1 20-ounce can tomatoes, drained
    and chopped

1 teaspoon salt
1/4 teaspoon freshly ground
    black pepper
1 8-ounce can tomato sauce
1 teaspoon oregano
1/4 teaspoon basil
liquid egg substitute = 1 egg
1/4 cup grated Parmesan cheese
1 tablespoon corn oil
1-1/2 cups (6 ounces) grated
    Mozzarella cheese

Makes 6 servings
Each serving contains:
3 protein portions
1 fat portion
264 calories
78 milligrams cholesterol

To pound the veal steak, place it on a wooden bread board and cover with wax paper or aluminum foil. Then, using a wooden mallet, pound the veal steak until it is about 1/8 inch thick. Slice the veal steak into 6 equal pieces and set aside.

Heat 1 tablespoon of corn oil in a large cured heavy iron skillet and add the garlic and onion. Sauté until they are a golden brown. Add the tomatoes, salt and pepper. Simmer, uncovered, for 15 minutes. Add the tomato sauce, oregano and basil and simmer over very low heat for 30 minutes.

While the vegetables are cooking, dip the veal steaks in the egg substitute and then dip them in the Parmesan cheese. Heat the remaining tablespoon corn oil in another heavy iron skillet and sauté the steaks over medium-high heat until they are golden brown on both sides and fork tender. Place the steaks in a 12 x 8-inch glass baking dish. Pour the tomato sauce over the veal steaks. Sprinkle the grated Mozzarella cheese evenly over the top. Bake uncovered in a 350° oven for 30 minutes.

MARINATED LAMB

1 leg of lamb, butterflied
1-1/2 tablespoons oregano
4 bay leaves, crushed
1/2 teaspoon freshly ground
    black pepper
1/4 cup red wine vinegar

4 garlic buds, crushed
1/2 cup soy sauce
2 cups dark Vermouth
2 cups Sherry
2 tablespoons corn oil

1 ounce lamb contains:
1 protein portion
73 calories
27.7 milligrams cholesterol
Calories added by marinade are
    negligible

Have your butcher bone and butterfly a leg of lamb. Remove all visible fat. Combine remaining ingredients and marinate lamb all day or overnight in the marinade. Then barbecue it over charcoal just like you would a steak. Serve it medium rare (good and pink).

VARIATION: Have the leg crosscut into thick lamb steaks.

BRAISED LAMB SHANKS IN MINT SAUCE

12 small, lean lamb shanks
1 teaspoon corn oil
1/2 cup water

2 cups Mint Sauce, page 43

Makes 6 servings

Each serving contains:
3 protein portions
219 calories
101 milligrams cholesterol

Remove fat from lamb shanks. Heat corn oil in a cured heavy iron skillet. When skillet is hot, add lamb shanks and brown well on all sides. When lamb shanks are brown, add water, cover and place in a 300° oven for 1-1/2 hours.

Remove from oven and pour Mint Sauce over the lamb shanks. Put cover back on skillet and return to the oven. Turn oven off and allow lamb to remain in oven for 30 minutes longer. Serve each guest 2 lamb shanks and spoon sauce over the top. I like Pine Nut Pilaf served with the lamb shanks.

bread, pasta, pancakes and such

I *love* to bake bread. I even like to make my own pasta! The main reason is that I am a show-off in the Hostess Department. There is nothing I like better at a dinner party than to mention *casually* that I baked all the bread myself. Or, even better, to tell my guests that I made the fettuccini noodles with my very own pasta machine.

Baking your own bread deserves greater importance than showing off, when you can make bread that is totally free of cholesterol, saturated fats, sugar *and* is also absolutely delicious! Also, the result, you may find, is better than anything you can buy.

BREAD CROUTONS AND BREAD CRUMBS

4 slices old bread

Makes 2 cups

Each 1/2 cup croutons contains:
1 starch portion

68 calories
0 cholesterol

If you do not have old bread, separate slices of fresh bread and leave them on a countertop for several hours, turning occasionally, until they can be cut up easily. Slice the bread in 1/4-inch squares. Place squares in a large shallow pan or on a cookie sheet, and put in a 300° oven for 20 minutes, or until a golden brown. Turn a few times so squares will brown evenly.

If you desire to make bread crumbs, you may either dry the bread 1 or 2 days until it is hard, or break it up into pieces and put it in the blender to make bread crumbs. If you wish toasted bread crumbs, put the toasted croutons in the blender.

TOASTED TORTILLA TRIANGLES

12 corn tortillas	6 tortilla triangles contain:	68 calories
salt	1 starch portion	0 cholesterol

Cut each tortilla into 6 pie-shaped pieces. Spread out half of the tortilla triangles on a cookie sheet and salt lightly. Bake them in a 400° oven for 10 minutes. Remove from oven, turn each one over and return them to the 400° oven for 3 more minutes. Place second half of tortilla triangles on cookie sheet and repeat process.

Toasted Tortilla Triangles are marvelous to serve with dips, with salads and soups, or crumbled up in casserole dishes. I like to serve them with my Taco Salad.

If you prefer smaller chips, cut the tortillas into smaller triangles before toasting them. They are so much fresher tasting than the tortilla chips you buy at the store and more importantly they are fat-free.

VARIATIONS: Sprinkle the tortillas with seasoned salts, cumin or chili powder for different flavors.

INDIAN CURRY BREAD

1 package dry yeast	liquid egg substitute = 1 egg	Makes 16 slices
1/4 cup warm water	1-1/2 tablespoons curry powder	Each slice contains:
1/2 pint small curd, creamed cottage cheese	1/2 teaspoon ground ginger	1 starch portion
sugar substitute = 2 tablespoons sugar	1/4 cup minced onion	68 calories
1 teaspoon salt	1/4 teaspoon baking soda	about 2.1 milligrams cholesterol
	2 cups all-purpose flour	

Soften yeast in warm water. Warm cottage cheese in saucepan. Add yeast and water mixture to the warm cottage cheese and mix well. Add the sugar substitute and salt to the egg substitute and mix. Combine the egg mixture with the cottage cheese. Add curry, ginger and onion to the cottage cheese mixture. Add the soda to the flour and add a little at a time to the other ingredients, mixing well. Cover and allow to stand at room temperature for several hours or until double in bulk. Stir dough until again reduced to its original size and put in a well-oiled and floured standard-size metal loaf pan. Cover the loaf pan and allow the dough to again double in bulk. Bake in a 350° oven for 45 minutes. Allow bread to cool to room temperature on a rack. It is much easier to slice when cool.

I think this bread is better the next day rather than right after it is baked! Wrap the bread in foil and store in the refrigerator until ready to use. Then, warm the bread or toast before serving.

bread, pasta, pancakes and such

THANKSGIVING BREAD

1 package dry yeast
1/4 cup warm water
1/2 pint small curd, creamed cottage
   cheese
liquid egg substitute = 1 egg
sugar substitute = 2 teaspoons sugar
1 teaspoon salt

1 teaspoon thyme
1/2 teaspoon sage
1/2 teaspoon rosemary
1/4 cup minced parsley
2 tablespoons minced onion
1/4 teaspoon baking soda
2 cups all-purpose flour

Makes 16 slices -
Each slice contains:
1 starch portion
68 calories
about 2.1 milligrams cholesterol

Soften yeast in warm water. Warm cottage cheese in saucepan. Add yeast and water mixture to the warm cottage cheese and mix well. Add the sugar substitute and salt to the egg substitute and mix. Combine the egg mixture with the cottage cheese. Crush the herbs, using a mortar and pestle and add to the cottage cheese mixture. Add the parsley and minced onion. Add the soda to the flour and add a little at a time to the other ingredients, mixing well.

Cover and allow to stand at room temperature for several hours or until double in bulk. Stir dough until again reduced to its original size and put in a well-oiled and floured standard-size metal loaf pan. Cover the loaf pan and allow the dough to again double in bulk. Bake in a 350° oven for 45 minutes. Allow bread to cool to room temperature on a rack. It is much easier to slice when cool.

I think this bread is better the next day rather than right after it is baked! Wrap the bread in foil and store in the refrigerator until ready to use. Then, warm the bread or toast before serving.

CINNAMON TOAST
(You start by making Cinnamon Bread!)

3 packages dry yeast
1/2 cup warm water
1 pint small curd, creamed cottage
   cheese
liquid egg substitute = 2 eggs
sugar substitute = 1-1/3 cups sugar
1 teaspoon salt

2 tablespoons ground cinnamon
2 tablespoons vanilla extract
4 cups all-purpose flour
1/2 teaspoon baking soda
1 cup raisins

Makes 2 loaves

Each loaf makes 16 slices
Each slice contains:
1 starch portion
1/4 fruit portion
78 calories
2 milligrams cholesterol

Soften yeast in warm water. Warm cottage cheese in a saucepan. Add yeast-water mixture to warm cottage cheese and mix well. Pour the liquid egg substitute in a bowl and add the sugar substitute, salt, cinnamon and vanilla and mix well. Combine the egg mixture with the cottage cheese mixture in a large mixing bowl. Add the soda to the flour and add a little at a time to the other ingredients, mixing well. Cover and allow to stand at room temperature for several hours, or until double in bulk.

Add raisins and stir dough until again reduced to its original size. Separate the dough into 2 equal halves and place each half in a well-oiled and floured, standard-size metal loaf pan. Cover the bread pans with a dish towel and allow dough to rise to again double in bulk. This takes about 1-1/2 hours. Bake in a 350° oven for 45 minutes. Cool bread on a rack, resting each loaf on its side.

It is much easier to slice when cool. When bread is cool, wrap it in foil or sealed plastic bags and refrigerate until ready to use. I like to refrigerate it at least 1 day before slicing it. Then, slice the bread as thinly as possible and toast under the broiler. This is your cinnamon toast!

bread, pasta, pancakes and such

FRENCH HERB BREAD
(They make it—you bake it!)

1/4 cup minced parsley
1/4 cup minced chives or green onion
   tops
1 teaspoon sweet basil, crushed
1/4 pound corn oil margarine,
   softened to room temperature

1 long loaf crusty French bread,
   unsliced (not sourdough)

Makes 16 slices

Each slice contains:
1 starch portion
1-1/2 fat portions
136 calories
0 cholesterol

Cream parsley, chives and basil into softened margarine, mixing thoroughly. Cut the loaf of bread into thirds lengthwise, and spread each section with one-third of the margarine mixture. Place thirds back together again and press firmly. Tightly wrap entire loaf in aluminum foil and refrigerate at least 24 hours before baking. Bake at 300° for 1 hour before serving. Unwrap and slice loaf crosswise into 3-inch-long sections. Serve hot and enjoy the raves about your "homemade bread." I think this is particularly tasty served with cold salads for lunch. Use your imagination!

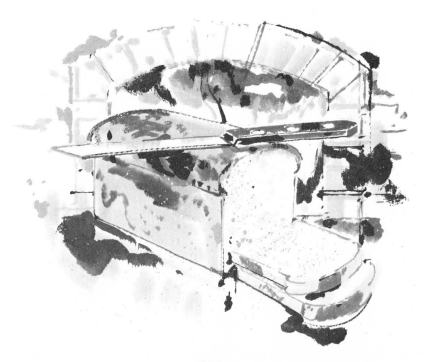

SAN FRANCISCO SOURDOUGH FRENCH TOAST

6 slices San Francisco sourdough bread
(If using the extra-large slices, use
3 slices cut in half)
liquid egg substitute = 4 eggs
1/4 cup buttermilk

1/4 cup low-fat milk
1/8 teaspoon salt
1 tablespoon corn oil margarine

Makes 6 servings

Each serving contains:
1 starch portion
3/4 protein portion
1/2 fat portion
146 calories
.7 milligram cholesterol

If possible, start the night before! Beat the egg substitute, buttermilk, low-fat milk and salt until well mixed. Place the 6 slices of bread in a flat baking dish. Pour the egg-substitute mixture over the bread. Pierce each slice of bread in several places with a fork. This will allow the bread to more readily absorb the egg mixture. Cover the dish and place in the refrigerator overnight.

In the morning, remove the bread from the baking dish and place it on an oiled or Teflon cookie sheet with sides. Pour any remaining liquid over the bread. Place the bread under the broiler until a golden brown in color. Turn the French toast over and brown the other side. Remove from broiler and lightly spread with corn oil margarine, about 1/2 teaspoon per serving. This is also good served with Applesauce or Strawberry Topping, Peach Jam, or use your imagination.

CAKE PAN BISCUITS OR SHORTCAKE

1-1/2 cups sifted all-purpose flour or
pre-sifted flour
2 teaspoons baking powder
1/2 teaspoon salt
4 tablespoons corn oil margarine,
softened

liquid egg substitute = 1 egg
1/3 cup low-fat milk

Makes 12 1/2-biscuit servings

Each 1/2 biscuit contains:
1 starch portion
1 fat portion
113 calories
Cholesterol negligible

Sift together flour, baking powder and salt. Blend with margarine using a pastry blender. Add egg substitute and blend with pastry blender. Add milk and mix with a large mixing spoon until thoroughly mixed. Oil and flour a 7-inch-square pan or casserole and spread dough evenly in the pan. Bake at 450° for 20 minutes. Cool slightly and cut into 6 equal servings. Using a spatula, carefully remove each rectangular-shaped biscuit and place on a rack. Split each biscuit in half horizontally.

bread, pasta, pancakes and such

BREAKFAST PIZZA

2 English muffins
2 teaspoons corn oil margarine
1 cup ricotta cheese
1 teaspoon ground cinnamon
1 teaspoon vanilla extract
sugar substitute = 1 tablespoon sugar

Makes 4 servings
Each serving contains:
1 starch portion
1 protein portion

1/2 fat portion
164 calories
With regular ricotta cheese:
29.1 milligrams cholesterol
With partly skimmed cheese:
18.2 milligrams cholesterol

Cut English muffins in half and roll with rolling pin until each half is flat and larger in diameter. Spread each muffin half with 1/2 teaspoon of margarine. Place under the broiler until a golden color. Mix ricotta cheese with the remaining ingredients and spread one-fourth of the mixture on each toasted muffin half. Place the muffins on a cookie sheet and bake in a 425° oven for about 8 minutes.

BUTTERMILK PANCAKES

liquid egg substitute = 2 eggs
1/4 teaspoon baking soda
1/4 teaspoon salt
2-1/2 teaspoons baking powder

1 cup buttermilk
1 cup all-purpose flour
1 teaspoon corn oil margarine

Makes 20 3-inch pancakes

Each pancake contains:
1 starch portion
68 calories
0 cholesterol

Beat the egg substitute, soda, salt and baking powder together with a beater until frothy. Add the buttermilk and flour. Mix well. Heat a cured heavy iron skillet or Teflon pan. Melt the margarine in the pan. When completely melted, wipe out the margarine using a paper towel. Use a large spoon and spoon out the batter into 3-inch pancakes. Cook over moderate heat until nicely brown on both sides.

MONTE CRISTO COUNTDOWN SANDWICH

2 teaspoons corn oil margarine
2 slices bread (I like sourdough best!)
2 slices ham substitute, cooked
1 slice Monterey Jack cheese
liquid egg substitute = 1 egg
2 tablespoons non-fat milk
1/8 teaspoon salt

Makes 1 sandwich
Each sandwich contains:
2 starch portions
3 protein portions
2 fat portions
445 calories
18 milligrams cholesterol

Each half sandwich contains:
1 starch portion
1-1/2 protein portions
1 fat portion
222 calories
9 milligrams cholesterol

Melt 1 teaspoon corn oil margarine in a cured heavy iron skillet. Spread the other teaspoon of corn oil margarine evenly on the 2 slices of bread. Place the 2 slices of ham substitute and the Jack cheese on 1 slice of the bread. Place the other slice of bread on top, to make a sandwich. Put the egg substitute and milk in a bowl, add the salt and whip the mixture with a fork. Dip the sandwich in the egg mixture, turning until all the egg mixture is absorbed into the bread. Place the sandwich in the heated skillet and cook until a rich golden brown on each side. I usually halve my sandwich and serve each half with 1/2 cup Peach Jam.

QUESADILLAS
(Mexican-style Melted Cheese Sandwiches)

8 corn tortillas
2 cups (1/2 pound) grated Monterey
    Jack cheese
1/4 teaspoon ground cumin
1/2 teaspoon salt

1 4-ounce can whole green chilies,
    seeded and chopped
2 tablespoons minced onion

Makes 8 quesadillas

Each quesadilla contains:
1 starch portion
1 protein portion
141 calories
18 milligrams cholesterol

Wrap the tortillas in aluminum foil and put in a 300° oven for 15 minutes so that they are warm and pliable. (Trying to fold tortillas straight from the refrigerator is impossible because they will break.) Remove tortillas from the oven and sprinkle each with 1/4 cup cheese. In a mixing bowl, mix together thoroughly the cumin, salt, chilies and onion. Evenly divide the mixture on each tortilla, spreading evenly over the cheese. Fold the tortilla in half and place in a flat, covered baking dish in a 350° oven for 15 minutes. Remove the Quesadillas from the oven and place on a cookie sheet. Put under the broiler for about 1-1/2 minutes per side to lightly brown each side and so the cheese will puff out on the edges.

bread, pasta, pancakes and such

PASTA VERDE
(For Fettuccini Verde)

2 cups all-purpose flour
liquid egg substitute = 2 eggs
1/2 teaspoon salt

1/2 cup well-drained, warm puréed
  spinach

1/2 cup cooked pasta contains:

1 starch portion
68 calories
0 cholesterol

In a large bowl, combine flour, egg substitute and salt. Using a pastry blender, blend until dough is thoroughly mixed. Add the warm puréed spinach a little at a time. At this point, the dough is most easily kneaded with your hands. Form a firm ball of dough and cover it with an inverted bowl for at least 1 hour. Then follow instructions for Basic Pasta, following.

BASIC PASTA

2 cups semolina flour (or all-purpose
  flour)
1-1/2 tablespoons corn oil

3/4 cup warm water

Makes 4 cups cooked pasta

1/2 cup cooked pasta contains:
1 starch portion
68 calories
0 cholesterol

Using a pastry blender, combine the flour and oil, cutting through it evenly until well mixed. Add water, a little at a time, to form a firm ball of dough. This process is best done by kneading by hand until dough becomes shiny, smooth and elastic. Cover the ball with an inverted bowl and allow to stand at room temperature for at least 1 hour. Then divide the ball of dough into 4 equal parts. Flatten each piece with the palm of your hand into a square-shaped section about 1 inch thick. With a heavy rolling pin, roll out dough lengthwise; turn, and roll out crosswise. Continue with this until you have pasta to desired thickness, usually about 1/8 inch thick, or less. Do this with each divided section of dough. To prevent sticking while rolling out the dough, carefully lift it and sprinkle a little more flour on the board.

For fettuccini, simply roll the thin pasta into jelly roll shape. Cut this into 1/4-inch slices and *quickly* unroll into strips to prevent them from sticking together.

To Make Pasta with Pasta Machine

Simply use a pastry blender and combine the flour and oil, cutting through it evenly until well-mixed. Add a little water at a time and form firm ball of dough. Then, pull off about one-third of the dough and feed through the rollers which have been set apart as far as possible.

Reroll the strip and, if it feels sticky, simply flour it lightly. When dough becomes shiny, smooth and elastic, kneading is completed. Then, place the strip through rollers, adjusting each time it is rolled to a narrower section until you have reached desired thickness for the pasta. When making fettuccini, put strip through the wide blades.

To Cook Pasta

Use a large kettle (8 quart) filled with water, adding 2 tablespoons of salt and 1 tablespoon of corn oil. Bring the water to a boil and add the pasta. Boil for approximately 5 minutes or to taste. Pasta should be what the Italians call *al dente,* meaning it has a slight resilience when eaten. Pasta made with semolina flour will take a couple of minutes longer to cook. Pour the water and pasta into a colander and drain well. The fettuccini is now ready to be mixed with your favorite sauce.

Different people make their own pasta for different reasons. I, personally, always make fresh pasta for fettuccini because it makes a tremendous difference in taste. *Plus,* nothing is more fun than making your own pasta when you have the time. I enjoy telling my friends that I made the pasta myself!

sweets and desserts

The best desserts for the happiness of your heart and the size of your waistline are fresh fruits in season, attractively presented. Of course, there are geographical regions in which it is difficult to obtain good fresh fruits during certain times of the year. When fresh fruits are not available, there are many canned, unsweetened fruits which make good substitutes.

However, there are other times, when either your sweet tooth or fond memories of a youth misspent in front of the neighborhood soda fountain get the best of you and you just plain don't want an apple or a dish of unsweetened applesauce. You *want* a chocolate sundae or a banana split! For any of those occasions, the following chapter should prove helpful in making those dreams possible.

HOT CURRIED FRUIT

4 tablespoons corn oil margarine
4 teaspoons curry powder
sugar substitute = 3 tablespoons sugar
1/2 teaspoon vanilla extract
1 1-pound can pear halves (water
   or juice packed, unsweetened)

1 1-pound can peach halves (water
   or juice packed, unsweetened)
1 1-pound can apricot halves (water
   or juice packed, unsweetened)
1 1-pound can pineapple chunks (water
   or juice packed, unsweetened)
1/2 cup Brandy
2 small bananas

Makes 12 servings
Each serving contains:
1 fruit portion
1 fat portion
85 calories
0 cholesterol

Preheat oven to 325°. Melt margarine and add curry powder, sugar substitute and vanilla. Drain pear and peach halves and cut each half into quarters. Drain apricot halves and pineapple chunks. Combine all fruits with melted margarine mixture and place in a 1-1/2-quart casserole. Bake, uncovered, for 30 minutes. During the last 10 minutes of baking time, add the Brandy. Remove casserole from the oven and cool to room temperature. Refrigerate for several hours or preferably overnight.

Before you plan to reheat and serve, remove the casserole from the refrigerator 1/2 hour ahead of time, and peel and slice the bananas, mixing thoroughly with the other curried fruits. Place in a 325° oven for approximately 15 minutes, or until thoroughly heated.

Obviously, this can be made and served immediately. If you do not have the time to chill and reheat, remove the casserole after it has cooked for 30 minutes. Add the sliced bananas and cook 10 more minutes before serving. Actually, it is much better if made ahead, as the flavors blend and mellow.

This is an excellent side dish for luncheons, served with cold meat or poultry. I have purposely used canned fruits for this dish because it gives you an unusual fruit dish which can be prepared when fresh fruits are not in season.

sweets and desserts

PEAR HELENA

3 large, ripe, firm pears
3 cups water
1 tablespoon vanilla extract
1/2 teaspoon ground cinnamon
sugar substitute = 1/3 cup sugar

Helena Sauce, following
2 teaspoons unsweetened powdered
   cocoa

Makes 6 servings
Each serving with 1/4 cup sauce
   contains:

1 fruit portion
1/2 fat portion
1/4 milk portion
115 calories
5 milligrams cholesterol

Peel pears carefully using an apple corer to remove the core from the end opposite the stem. Slice each pear in half using a small paring knife to remove any of the core still left in the pears. Put the water and all other ingredients except cocoa in a saucepan and bring to a slow boil. Place pears in simmering water and cook about 10 minutes, or until easily pierced with a fork but not soft. Remove pears from heat and let cool to room temperature in the sauce. Cover and refrigerate all day or overnight in the sauce.

To serve, place each pear cut side down on a plate or in a shallow bowl and spoon the Helena Sauce over the top. Then sprinkle each serving with 1/3 teaspoon cocoa.

HELENA SAUCE

1-1/2 cups Basic White Sauce, page 38   sugar substitute = 1 tablespoon sugar   1-1/2 teaspoons vanilla extract

Mix Basic White Sauce with sugar substitute and vanilla, using a wire whisk. Spoon evenly over each serving.

VARIATION: This sauce is excellent on any poached fruit. I even like it on fresh strawberries. Fruit portion and calories remain the same.

EFFIE'S BAKED APPLESAUCE

3 large green cooking apples
3/4 cup water
sugar substitute = 1-1/2 tablespoons
   sugar

1/4 teaspoon ground nutmeg
1/4 teaspoon ground cinnamon
1/2 teaspoon vanilla extract

Makes 2 cups

Each 1/2 cup contains:
1 fruit portion
40 calories
0 cholesterol

Wash and peel apples. Dice into 1-inch cubes, removing the core completely. Mix all other ingredients in the water. Place the diced apples in a glass loaf pan or baking dish. (I prefer a loaf pan because the apples stay more moist.) Pour the water mixture over the apples. Bake, uncovered, at 325° for 45 minutes. Remove from oven and allow baked apples to come to room temperature. Store in the refrigerator.

This applesauce is an excellent accompaniment to many meats. It's a good breakfast fruit, a light dessert and the basic ingredient for Applesauce Topping.

VARIATION: If you prefer a smooth, creamy applesauce, put the baked apples in a blender a few at a time and blend until smooth. Add all the liquid from the apples. If necessary, add 1/4 cup more water to make a creamier consistency.

APPLESAUCE TOPPING

2 cups Effie's Baked Applesauce,
   preceding
1/4 cup water
1/4 teaspoon ground cinnamon

1 teaspoon vanilla extract
sugar substitute = 1 teaspoon sugar

Makes 2 cups

Each 1/2 cup contains:
1 fruit portion
40 calories
0 cholesterol

Place all ingredients in blender and blend until smooth. This is a marvelous sauce with a wide variety of uses. It is fabulous over Cinnamon Soufflé. It is also good on pancakes, French toast and blintzes.

sweets and desserts

PRUNE MOUSSE

12 dried prunes
3/4 cup boiling water
1-1/2 cups low-fat Jelled Milk, page 39
sugar substitute = 1 tablespoon sugar

1 teaspoon vanilla extract
1/4 teaspoon almond extract

Makes 6 servings
Each serving contains:

1 fruit portion
1/4 milk portion
72 calories
3.9 milligrams cholesterol

Put the prunes in a bowl and pour the boiling water over them. Cover immediately and allow to come to room temperature. Refrigerate for 24 hours. Remove prunes from refrigerator. Pour the water in which they have been soaking in the blender. Remove pits from prunes and add to blender. Add all other ingredients and blend on high speed until frothy. Pour mixture into an oiled 4-cup crown mold (or 6 individual molds) and refrigerate for at least 3 hours.

To unmold, tap the bottom of the mold and place a plate over the top. Invert *quickly* in an even movement to unmold the mousse on the plate. Garnish with a dab of Whoopee Whipped Cream or Rum Custard Sauce—or it's good as is!

POACHED PEACH MOUSSE

For Poaching:
6 medium-size peaches, peeled and
   diced
2 cups water
1-1/2 teaspoons vanilla extract
1 cinnamon stick, broken in half

For Mousse:
1/3 cup water
2 envelopes unflavored gelatin
1-1/2 cups low-fat milk
1-1/2 teaspoons vanilla extract
sugar substitute = 1/3 cup sugar
1/4 teaspoon ground cinnamon

Makes 6 servings
Each serving contains:
1 fruit portion
1/4 milk portion
103 calories
3.9 milligrams cholesterol

Put the diced peaches, water, vanilla and broken pieces of cinnamon stick into a saucepan. Bring to a boil. Reduce the heat and simmer 5 minutes. Remove the peaches from the heat and allow to cool at room temperature. Cover and refrigerate peaches in liquid until cold.

While peaches are cooling, soften the unflavored gelatin in the 1/3 cup of water for 5 minutes. Heat the gelatin mixture, stirring constantly, until all the gelatin is dissolved. *Do not boil.* Add the low-fat milk to the gelatin mixture and refrigerate until firm. By jelling the milk while cooling the peaches, the 2 main ingredients for your mousse will be ready about the same time.

When the peaches are cold, remove the cinnamon sticks and drain off the liquid, reserving 1/2 cup. Put the 1/2 cup of poaching liquid, vanilla, sugar substitute and cinnamon in the blender. Add the jelled milk and half of the poached peaches (about 1-1/4 cups) and blend at high speed until frothy, about 3 minutes. Remove from blender and combine this mixture with the remaining half of the poached peaches and mix thoroughly. Pour the entire mixture into an oiled 6-cup mold and refrigerate for 3 to 4 hours, or until very firm. To unmold, tap the bottom of the mold and place a plate over the top. Invert *quickly* in an even movement to unmold the mousse on the plate.

This is a light, low-calorie dessert which I even like for breakfast! Serve it with cottage cheese for the protein. When fresh peaches are not in season, this recipe can be made with canned, unsweetened peaches. This eliminates the poaching step, because you use the peaches directly from the can.

sweets and desserts

PINEAPPLE BOATS WITH "COCONUT" SAUCE

1 fresh pineapple	Makes 4 pineapple boats	1 fruit portion
1 cup Coconut Sauce, following	Each serving of pineapple and 1/4 cup	1/4 milk portion
ground cinnamon	sauce contains:	70 calories
		3.9 milligrams cholesterol

Cut the pineapple lengthwise into quarters, carefully cutting through the green leaves at the top to leave a section of leaves on each pineapple quarter. Using a very sharp small paring knife, carefully cut each corner of the pineapple quarter from its shell. It is necessary to cut down both sides of the pineapple section. Cut the hard top core section of the pineapple off and discard it. Cut the piece of pineapple sitting on its shell in half lengthwise, then cut horizontally into bite-size pieces. Top each pineapple boat with Coconut Sauce and sprinkle lightly with cinnamon. Beautiful, delicious and low calorie!

COCONUT SAUCE

1/2 cup low-fat Jelled Milk, page 39	1/2 teaspoon vanilla extract	sugar substitute = 2 teaspoons sugar
1/2 cup low-fat milk, cold	1/2 teaspoon coconut extract	

Put all ingredients in blender and blend until smooth. Allow to stand a few minutes to thicken before spooning over the pineapple boats.

sweets and desserts

BAKED BANANAS

6 ripe bananas
1 tablespoon corn oil margarine
sugar substitute = 1/3 cup sugar

2 teaspoons peeled and grated ginger
   root, or
1 teaspoon powdered ginger

Makes 6 servings

Each serving contains:
2 fruit portions
1/2 fat portion
103 calories
0 cholesterol

Remove a strip of the banana peel 1 inch wide lengthwise down the side of each banana. Arrange the bananas open side up in a shallow baking dish. Melt the margarine in a saucepan and add sugar substitute and ginger. Mix thoroughly. Brush the melted margarine mixture over the exposed part of the banana. Loosen the peel slightly on both sides of the opening and brush a little of the mixture under the peel, using a pastry brush. Bake in a 350° oven for 15 to 20 minutes, depending on the size of the bananas.

These bananas are an unusual accompaniment to cold meat or egg dishes for brunch or lunch. They also make unusual desserts. When serving them for dessert, I put a little Whoopee Whipped Cream on top of each banana and sprinkle it lightly with cinnamon.

OLD-FASHIONED STRAWBERRY SHORTCAKE

4 cups fresh strawberries, all sliced
   except 8 left whole
sugar substitute to taste
4 Cake Pan Shortcakes, page 127, split

2 cups Whoopee Whipped Cream,
   page 149

Makes 8 servings
Each serving contains:

1 starch portion
1 fat portion
1/2 fruit portion
133 calories
1.5 milligrams cholesterol

Place sliced strawberries in a large bowl and sweeten to taste with sugar substitute. Place each shortcake half in a shallow bowl and cover with a 1/2 cup of the sliced strawberries. Spoon 4 tablespoons of the Whoopee Whipped Cream on the top. Garnish top of each serving with a whole strawberry.

CINNAMON SOUFFLÉ

2-1/2 tablespoons all-purpose flour
1 cup low-fat milk, at boiling point
6 eggs, separated, at room temperature
2 tablespoons corn oil
sugar substitute = 1/3 cup sugar
1 tablespoon ground cinnamon

1 tablespoon vanilla extract
1-1/2 cups low-fat cottage cheese,
  blended until smooth and
  creamy in texture
1/8 teaspoon salt
1/8 teaspoon cream of tartar

Makes 12 servings for dessert,
  6 servings for brunch
Each dessert serving contains:
1 protein portion
73 calories
44.6 milligrams cholesterol

Measure out the flour in a small bowl. Put the milk in a saucepan on medium heat. (This will have it at the boiling point when you need it.) Separate the eggs, putting the yolks in a separate dish and reserving 2 of the yolks to be used in the recipe. Place the remaining 4 egg yolks in a dish for your pet! Heat the oil in a large saucepan over medium heat. Add the flour and stir constantly for about 3 minutes, being careful not to brown flour. When the milk starts to boil, remove the oil and flour from heat temporarily and pour the boiling mixture into the oil and flour mixture all at once, rapidly mixing with a wire whisk. Put the milk mixture back on low heat and continue stirring with a whisk until the mixture has returned to a slow boil and thickens (this does not take very long). Remove from heat and add yolks one at a time, mixing thoroughly after each egg yolk is added. Then, add the sugar substitute, cinnamon and vanilla. Mix thoroughly. Add the 1-1/2 cups of smooth, blended, low-fat cottage cheese and again mix thoroughly.

At this point, you can stop the soufflé and wait to proceed until ready to serve it. I often do this portion of the soufflé early in the afternoon. If I plan to use it as a dessert for dinner that evening, I combine the soufflé base with the egg whites between courses of the dinner and serve it for dessert. Or, if you are using this soufflé as the main course for a brunch, you can make the base early in the morning and cook it just prior to seating your guests at the table. If you make the base so far ahead that it is cold by the time you are ready to use it, warm it to lukewarm before proceeding.

Preheat oven to 400°. Add salt and cream of tartar to 6 egg whites at room temperature. Beat the egg whites until they are stiff, *but not dry*—they should hold firm peaks! Mix one-third of the egg whites into the soufflé base to lighten the mix. Carefully fold the remaining egg whites into the mixture, being very careful not to overmix. Pour the entire mix into a 9-inch soufflé dish and place soufflé in the 400° oven. Close the door and *immediately* turn the heat down to 375°. Cook for 30 minutes, or until soufflé is billowing and lightly brown. It can be cooked for longer than this if you prefer a more solid-textured soufflé. I, personally, like the center of a soufflé quite soft.

This soufflé can be served by itself, or with a variety of toppings. I like it best with Applesauce Topping spooned over each serving. It is also delightful with fresh fruit in season, such as strawberries, peaches and pineapple. Always remember, soufflés are to be served *immediately.* If necessary, make your guests *wait* for the soufflé; the soufflé will *not wait* for your guests. It will literally fall on its face!

sweets and desserts

MINT MIST

2 cups low-fat Jelled Milk, page 39
1/2 cup low-fat milk
1-1/4 teaspoons vanilla extract
1/4 teaspoon mint extract

sugar substitute = 1 tablespoon sugar
2 drops green food coloring
1 teaspoon unsweetened powdered
   cocoa

Makes 5 1/2-cup servings

Each serving contains:
1/2 milk portion
63 calories
7.7 milligrams cholesterol

Put all the ingredients except cocoa into a blender and blend for 2 minutes on very high speed, or until frothy. Pour into a large bowl, cover and place in the refrigerator for at least 2 hours before serving. To serve, spoon into 5 sherbet glasses and sprinkle top of each serving with cocoa. If possible, garnish with fresh mint sprig.

AMBROSIA

1-1/2 cups chopped, unsweetened
   fresh or canned pineapple
1-1/2 small bananas, peeled and sliced
1 teaspoon freshly squeezed lemon
   juice
2 cups low-fat Jelled Milk, page 39

1 teaspoon vanilla extract
1 teaspoon coconut extract
1/2 teaspoon strawberry extract
sugar substitute = 1 tablespoon sugar
3 drops red food coloring

Makes 4 servings
Each serving contains:
1-1/2 fruit portions
1/2 milk portion
123 calories
7.7 milligrams cholesterol

Mash pineapple with a fork. Put the pineapple in a saucepan and bring it to a boil. Reduce heat and simmer for 5 minutes. Remove from heat and cool to room temperature. Put the sliced bananas in a blender. Add lemon juice and blend to mix. Add the cooled pineapple and all other ingredients. Blend until frothy. Pour into a bowl or 4 individual sherbet glasses and refrigerate until firm before serving. This is both good and pretty served with Whoopee Whipped Cream.

CHOCOLATE SUNDAE

3 cups Happy Heart Ice Cream, page 144
1 recipe Chocolate Sauce, page 149
2 tablespoons Toasted Almond Flakes,
   page 45
6 strawberries (optional)

Makes 6 servings
Each serving contains:

1 milk portion
1/2 fat portion
1/2 starch portion
182 calories
15.5 milligrams cholesterol

Put 1/2 cup Happy Heart Ice Cream in each of 6 sherbet glasses. Divide Chocolate Sauce evenly on top of each serving. Sprinkle 1 teaspoon of Toasted Almond Flakes on each serving and place a strawberry on top for garnish, if desired.

BANANA SPLIT

3 cups Happy Heart Ice Cream,
   page 144
3 small bananas
1 recipe Chocolate Sauce, page 149
1-1/2 cups Strawberry Topping,
   page 148

2 tablespoons Toasted Almond Flakes,
   page 45
6 strawberries (optional)

Makes 6 servings
Each serving contains:

1 milk portion
1/2 fat portion
3/4 fruit portion
1/2 starch portion
212 calories
15.5 milligrams cholesterol

Place 2 scoops of Happy Heart Ice Cream in each of 6 banana split dishes (corn dishes work beautifully, too). Slice each banana in quarters lengthwise. Place a banana quarter on each side of each dish. Divide the Chocolate Sauce evenly over 1 of the scoops of ice cream in each of the dishes. Pour 1/4 cup Strawberry Topping over the top of the remaining scoops of ice cream. Sprinkle 1 teaspoon Toasted Almond Flakes over top of each banana split. Slice the strawberries in half and place a strawberry half on top of each scoop of ice cream.

sweets and desserts

HAPPY HEART ICE CREAM

1-1/2 teaspoons unflavored gelatin
2 tablespoons water
1 cup canned skim milk
1 tablespoon cornstarch
2 cups low-fat milk

2 teaspoons vanilla extract
sugar substitute = 1/3 cup sugar
2 egg whites
dash of salt
1/8 teaspoon cream of tartar

Makes 1 quart
1/2 cup contains:
1/2 milk portion
52 calories
7.7 milligrams cholesterol

Put the gelatin in the water and allow to soften. Pour 3/4 cup of the canned skim milk in the top of a double boiler. Add the cornstarch to the remaining 1/4 cup of canned milk and mix until thoroughly dissolved. Add the cornstarch mixture to the double boiler. Heat milk and cornstarch over simmering water until it comes to a boil, stirring constantly. Allow the mixture to simmer for about 3 minutes, or until slightly thickened.

Remove from heat and add softened gelatin. Mix until all gelatin is completely dissolved. Add the low-fat milk, vanilla and sugar substitute. Mix thoroughly. Place mixture in the refrigerator for at least 2 hours, or until thoroughly chilled. Then, in a separate bowl, put the egg whites, salt and cream of tartar. Beat the egg whites until stiff but not dry and fold into the chilled mixture. Pour mixture into your ice cream maker and proceed according to the directions of your own ice cream maker. Note the low calorie content. See why I recommend making your own ice cream!

HAPPY HEART PEACH ICE CREAM

3/4 teaspoon unflavored gelatin	1 teaspoon vanilla extract	Makes 1 quart
1 tablespoon water	sugar substitute = 3 tablespoons sugar	Each 1/2 cup contains:
1/2 cup canned skim milk	1 egg white	1/4 milk portion
1-1/2 teaspoons cornstarch	dash of salt	1/2 fruit portion
1 cup low-fat milk	1/4 teaspoon cream of tartar	46 calories
	1-1/2 cups mashed, fresh peaches	2.2 milligrams cholesterol

Put the gelatin in the water and allow to soften. Pour the canned milk in a saucepan; add the cornstarch and mix thoroughly. Then, heat over moderate heat (or use a double boiler) until it comes to the boiling point. Simmer slowly, stirring with a wire whisk until slightly thickened. Remove pan from heat and add softened gelatin. Mix until all gelatin is completely dissolved. Add the low-fat milk, vanilla and sugar substitute and mix thoroughly. Place mixture in the refrigerator for at least 2 hours or until thoroughly chilled.

In a separate bowl, put the egg white, salt and cream of tartar and beat until stiff but not dry. Fold into the chilled mixture. Add the mashed peaches and mix thoroughly. Pour the mixture into ice cream maker and proceed according to its directions.

RAISIN-RICE PUDDING

2 cups cooked rice
2 cups non-fat milk
liquid egg substitute = 4 eggs
sugar substitute = 1/4 cup sugar
1 tablespoon ground cinnamon

2 teaspoons vanilla extract
1 cup raisins

Makes 8 servings
Each serving contains:

1/2 starch portion
1/4 milk portion
1/2 protein portion
1 fruit portion
119 calories
.65 milligram cholesterol

Combine all ingredients, mixing well. Pour into a casserole and set the casserole in a larger, deep pan. Add boiling water to a depth of 3/4 inch. Bake at 350° for 1 hour and 15 minutes. For parties, I put the pudding in an oiled fancy 6-cup mold (instead of a casserole). Chill it well and unmold on a plate before serving. It's even prettier decorated with Whoopee Whipped Cream.

COTTAGE CUSTARD

1-1/2 cups non-fat milk
liquid egg substitute = 2 eggs
1-1/2 teaspoons vanilla extract
1/2 teaspoon ground nutmeg

sugar substitute = 1/4 cup sugar
1/2 pint low-fat cottage cheese

Makes 6 servings
Each serving contains:

1/4 milk portion
1 protein portion
93 calories
2.4 milligrams cholesterol

Put all ingredients in the blender and blend until smooth. Pour mixture into 6 custard cups. Place custard cups in a pan of boiling water to a depth of 3/4 inch. Place the pan in a 350° oven and bake for 1 hour. Remove pan and allow to cool to room temperature. Tightly cover each custard cup and store in the refrigerator. I love this custard for breakfast with fresh fruit.

VARIATION: Substitute cinnamon for nutmeg. (I like this better!) Also you can use other extracts such as rum, coconut and almond in place of the vanilla. I like rum and coconut combined and pineapple served with the custard.

RUM CUSTARD SAUCE

1-1/2 cups low-fat milk
liquid egg substitute = 2 eggs
1/4 teaspoon salt
sugar substitute = 1/3 cup sugar

1/2 teaspoon vanilla extract
1 teaspoon rum extract

Makes 2 cups sauce
Each cup contains:

3/4 milk portion
1 protein portion
167 calories
11.6 milligrams cholesterol

Bring milk to the boiling point in the top of a double boiler over simmering water. Beat together egg substitute and salt. Slowly pour hot milk into egg mixture, stirring with a wire whisk. Return mixture to double boiler and continue cooking over simmering water until custard coats a metal spoon. Remove from heat and cool. Add sugar substitute and rum and vanilla extracts and mix thoroughly.

VARIATIONS: Substitute other extracts for rum, such as coconut, maple, brandy or lemon; my favorite variation is to use 1-1/2 teaspoons vanilla extract without the rum.

sweets and desserts

PEACH JAM

2 cups fresh peaches, peeled and sliced
1 teaspoon freshly squeezed lemon
   juice
1 cinnamon stick

1 teaspoon unflavored gelatin
1 tablespoon water
1/2 teaspoon vanilla extract
sugar substitute = 2 tablespoons sugar

Makes 1-1/2 cups

Each 1/2 cup contains:
1 fruit portion
40 calories
0 cholesterol

Put the peaches in a saucepan and sprinkle lemon juice over them. Break the cinnamon stick in half and add to the peaches. Cook, covered, over very low heat without water for about 20 minutes. Remove the lid and bring juice to the boiling point. Boil for 1 minute and remove from heat. Soften the gelatin in the water. Pour the hot juice from the peaches into the softened gelatin mixture and stir until gelatin is completely dissolved. Add the dissolved gelatin and vanilla to the peaches. Allow to cool to room temperature. Remove the cinnamon stick. Add the sugar substitute, mix well and refrigerate.

STRAWBERRY TOPPING

2 cups fresh or fresh frozen unsweetened strawberries
1 teaspoon freshly squeezed
   lemon juice

1/2 cup water
1 tablespoon arrowroot
sugar substitute = 1/4 cup sugar

Makes 2 cups

Each cup contains:
1 fruit portion
40 calories
0 cholesterol

Put the strawberries in a heavy saucepan. Cook, covered, over very low heat, about 10 minutes. Remove the lid and bring to the boiling point. Boil for 1 minute and remove from heat. Add the lemon juice and mix well.

Combine the water and arrowroot and bring to a boil. Simmer until clear and slightly thickened, about 2 minutes. Remove from heat and cool to room temperature. Add the sugar substitute to the arrowroot mixture and mix well. Combine the arrowroot and strawberries and again mix well. Cool to room temperature and store in the refrigerator. This topping is excellent on ice cream or used like jam on French toast, pancakes, et cetera.

WHOOPEE WHIPPED CREAM

1 cup canned skim milk, very cold
1 teaspoon vanilla extract
sugar substitute = 2 tablespoons sugar

Makes a scant 5 cups of whipped
   topping
Each 1/2 cup contains:

approximately 20 calories
1.5 milligrams cholesterol

Chill the mixing bowl and beaters in the freezer. When ready to whip, add all ingredients to the chilled bowl, using either an egg beater or an electric mixer. Beat the mixture until desired consistency. I like it to form firm peaks. Serve *immediately,* because this whipped topping does not remain firm for very long.

If you are wondering why I make my whipped topping with canned skim milk rather than non-fat dry milk which has half the calories, it is because the non-fat dry milk takes much longer to whip and retains its whipped consistency for a far shorter time. Also, the dry milk requires lemon juice to help whip it, and I do not like the lemon juice flavor in whipped cream.

CHOCOLATE SAUCE

1-1/2 cups low-fat milk
2 tablespoons corn oil margarine
1/2 cup unsweetened powdered cocoa
1/8 teaspoon salt

sugar substitute = 1 cup sugar

Makes 6 servings
Each serving contains:

1/2 milk portion
1 fat portion
1/2 starch portion
142 calories
7.7 milligrams cholesterol

Measure the milk into a saucepan and put on medium heat so that it will be at the boiling point when you need it. In another saucepan, melt the margarine and add the cocoa, mixing thoroughly. Allow the cocoa and margarine to cook for about 3 minutes. *Do not brown.* Remove from heat and add the boiling milk all at once, rapidly stirring the mixture with a wire whisk. Put back on medium heat and bring back to a simmer. Simmer, continuing to stir with the whisk until the sauce reaches the desired thickness (this varies with how you plan to use the sauce). Remove from heat and cool slightly. Add the salt and sugar substitute and mix thoroughly.

I like this sauce exactly as it is because I use it primarily for making a chocolate sundae. If you want to use this sauce for a hot chocolate sundae, you should make it just before you plan to serve it, as the sugar substitute tends to take on a bitter taste when reheated.

sweets and desserts

GRAHAM CRACKER PIE CRUST AND TOPPING

16 graham crackers
4 tablespoons corn oil margarine,
  softened

Makes 1 pie crust; 8 servings

Entire pie crust contains:
8 starch portions
12 fat portions
1,084 calories
0 cholesterol

Each serving contains:
1 starch portion
1-1/2 fat portions
136 calories
0 cholesterol

Roll the graham crackers with a rolling pin until they are in fine crumbs. To save time, put the graham crackers in a large plastic baggie and roll them, thus eliminating much mess! Put the graham cracker crumbs in a bowl and add the softened margarine. Using a pastry blender, mix the graham crackers with the margarine until completely mixed and the consistency of dough. Reserve 2 tablespoons of this mixture to use later.

Place the remaining mixture, evenly spread, on the bottom of a 9-inch pie plate. Place the 2 tablespoons of the reserved mixture in another ovenproof dish to be baked at the same time as the crust to be used sprinkled on top of the pie. Put both the pie plate and plate of crumbs in a 375° oven and bake for 8 minutes. Cool the pie crust to room temperature before adding filling.

GRASSHOPPER PIE

Graham Cracker Pie Crust and Topping,
  preceding, omitting 2 of the crackers
  and adding 2-1/2 tablespoons unsweetened powdered cocoa
1/3 cup water

2 envelopes unflavored gelatin
2 cups low-fat milk
1-1/2 teaspoons vanilla extract
1/8 teaspoon mint extract
2 drops green food coloring
sugar substitute = 3 tablespoons sugar

Makes 8 servings

Each serving of filling and crust
  contains:
1 starch portion
1/4 milk portion
1-1/2 fat portions
167 calories
3.9 milligrams cholesterol

Prepare and bake the crust and topping as directed, adding the cocoa to the graham cracker crumbs before combining with the margarine. Allow crust to cool to room temperature.

Put the water in a saucepan and add the gelatin. Allow the gelatin to soften in the water for at least 5 minutes. Heat the gelatin mixture over low heat, stirring constantly until gelatin is completely dissolved. Add the low-fat milk to the gelatin mixture and mix thoroughly. Place in the refrigerator for about 30 minutes, or until mixture starts to thicken. Remove from the refrigerator and place in a blender. Add the vanilla extract, mint extract, green food coloring and sugar substitute. Blend until a foamy consistency. Pour filling into the cooled pie shell. Sprinkle reserved cooked crumbs over the top evenly and place pie in refrigerator to chill for at least 3 hours before serving. If possible, make a day ahead of time.

BANANA CREAM PIE

Graham Cracker Pie Crust and
Topping, page 150, using a
10-inch pie plate
1-1/2 cups low-fat milk
liquid egg substitute = 2 eggs
1/4 teaspoon salt
1 envelope unflavored gelatin
1/4 cup water

sugar substitute = 1/3 cup sugar
1-1/2 teaspoons vanilla extract
4 small bananas (or 3 medium, or
2 large)
2 tablespoons freshly squeezed
lemon juice

Makes 8 servings

Each serving filling and crust contains:
1 starch portion
1-1/2 fat portions
1/4 protein portion
1/2 fruit portion
174 calories
2.9 milligrams cholesterol

Bring the milk to the boiling point in the top of a double boiler over simmering water. Beat the egg substitute with the salt. Slowly pour the hot milk into the egg mixture, stirring with a wire whisk. Return the mixture to the double boiler and continue cooking over simmering water until custard coats a metal spoon. Remove from the heat. Soften the gelatin in the water and add to the hot custard, stirring until the gelatin is completely dissolved. Cool this mixture to room temperature and add the vanilla and sugar substitute. Mix thoroughly.

Peel the bananas and dice them. Place in a bowl and sprinkle with lemon juice and mix thoroughly. Put 1/2 of the diced bananas in a 10-inch graham cracker pie shell. Using a fork or pastry blender, mix the remaining 1/2 of the bananas and add them to the custard, mixing thoroughly. Pour the banana custard over the diced bananas in the pie shell. Sprinkle the reserved cooked graham cracker crumbs over the top of the pie. Chill at least 3 hours before serving.

sweets and desserts

SESAME SEED COOKIES

1/2 cup sesame seeds
1/4 pound corn oil margarine, softened
1-1/2 cups all-purpose flour
sugar substitute = 2/3 cup sugar
1 teaspoon baking powder

1/8 teaspoon salt
1 tablespoon vanilla extract
liquid egg substitute = 1 egg

Makes 36 cookies

Each cookie contains:
1 fat portion
1/4 starch portion
62 calories
0 cholesterol

Place sesame seeds in a 350° oven for 15 minutes, or until a golden brown in color. Cool before using. Put the margarine in a large mixing bowl and allow to soften. Combine the flour, sugar substitute, baking powder and salt. Mix well. Add the flour mixture to the softened margarine and mix thoroughly, using a pastry blender.

Combine the vanilla and egg substitute and mix well. Add to the flour mixture and mix thoroughly. Add the toasted sesame seeds and again mix thoroughly. The dough will be stiff and difficult to mix. When it is thoroughly mixed, make small, thin cookies, no larger than 2 inches in diameter, and space evenly on ungreased cookie sheets. Bake in a 350° oven for approximately 20 minutes. Cool and carefully remove with spatula to serving plate.

CHOCOLATE MINT DROP COOKIES

3/4 cup corn oil margarine, softened
1-1/2 cups all-purpose flour
1/2 cup unsweetened powdered cocoa
sugar substitute = 3/4 cup sugar
1 teaspoon baking powder

1/4 teaspoon salt
1 tablespoon vanilla extract
1/2 teaspoon mint extract
liquid egg substitute = 1 egg

Makes 48 cookies

Each 2 cookies contain:
1-1/2 fat portions
1/2 starch portion
102 calories
0 cholesterol

Put the margarine in a large mixing bowl and allow to soften. Combine the flour, cocoa, sugar substitute, baking powder and salt. Mix well. Add the flour mixture to the softened margarine and mix thoroughly, using a pastry blender.

Combine the vanilla, mint extract and liquid egg substitute and mix well. Add to the flour mixture and mix thoroughly. The dough will be stiff and difficult to mix. When it is thoroughly mixed, make cookies 1-1/2 inches in diameter (size of a silver dollar) and space evenly on ungreased cookie sheets. Bake in a 350° oven for approximately 15 minutes. Cool and carefully remove with spatula to serving plate.

beverages

I am certainly not attempting to write a bartender's guide in this section but, when a drink lends itself particularly well to a deliciously different cocktail, I mention it. My reason is to give greater variety of use to some of the recipes in this chapter. For example: A Robinson Crusoe Fizz is the favorite among my teen-age son's friends for an after-school refreshment. With the addition of a little rum or vodka it is also the favorite brunch fizz among my own "non teen-age" friends. Many of these beverages also make great toppings for fruit, cereal, custard or ice cream. I urge you to experiment with my recipes in this chapter and to invent new drinks of your own. In this way you can find a healthy, happy approach to children's snack time, too!

FRESH GRAPEFRUIT FRAPPÉ

1 peeled, sectioned fresh grapefruit	Makes 6 servings	1 fruit portion
2 cups freshly squeezed grapefruit juice	Each serving contains:	40 calories
		0 cholesterol

When peeling and sectioning the grapefruit, be very careful to remove all of the membrane from each grapefruit section, otherwise this will add a pithy texture and taste to the drink. Put the grapefruit sections in the blender with the grapefruit juice and blend until frothy. Pour into chilled glasses over ice.

beverages

ROBINSON CRUSOE FIZZ

1 small banana, peeled and sliced
1 teaspoon freshly squeezed lemon
juice
1 cup unsweetened pineapple juice
1/2 cup crushed fresh or canned
unsweetened pineapple

2 cups cold non-fat milk
1 teaspoon vanilla extract
1/2 teaspoon strawberry extract
1 teaspoon coconut extract
2 drops red food coloring
sugar substitute = 1 tablespoon sugar
1/2 cup crushed ice

Makes 4 servings
Each serving contains:
1-1/2 fruit portions
1/2 milk portion
100 calories
7.7 milligrams cholesterol

Put sliced banana in blender. Add lemon juice and blend to mix. Put all other ingredients in blender with banana and blend until frothy. Serve in tall chilled glasses.

In my opinion this is not only the best brunch drink (either as the recipe is given or with the addition of gin, vodka or rum) I have ever tasted, but it makes a fabulous topping for fresh fruit of all types. I particularly like it poured over a combination of diced fresh melon and papaya. Use your imagination and the fresh fruit available.

BANANA BLIZZARD

3 small bananas, peeled and sliced
2 teaspoons freshly squeezed lemon
juice
1-1/2 cups cold buttermilk
1-1/2 cups cold non-fat milk

sugar substitute = 4 teaspoons sugar
1/2 teaspoon vanilla extract
1/2 cup crushed ice

Makes 6 servings

Each serving contains:
1 fruit portion
1/2 milk portion
80 calories
2.4 milligrams cholesterol

Put sliced banana in blender. Add lemon juice and blend to mix. Put all remaining ingredients in blender with banana and blend on high speed until frothy. Serve in chilled glasses. I personally like this poured over cereal for breakfast. It's a deliciously different way to add fruit to your cereal.

MINT RIVER

4 cups firmly packed, chopped
    fresh mint leaves and stems
4 cups water

sugar substitute to taste
2 drops green food coloring

Makes 1 quart
Free food, calories negligible
0 cholesterol

Put mint and water in a saucepan and bring to a boil. Remove from heat and allow to stand for 30 minutes. Strain liquid from mint. Cover tightly and refrigerate until cold. When thoroughly chilled, sweeten to taste with sugar substitute. Add the 2 drops of green food coloring. Serve over crushed ice for a delightfully refreshing drink!

VARIATIONS: *Mint Phosphate* Add a dash of soda water to make this refreshing drink even more refreshing! *Mint Rapids* Add vodka for a sensational new Southern cocktail!

LATE-DATE NIGHTCAP

3 cups low-fat milk
16 dates, pitted and chopped
sugar substitute = 1 teaspoon sugar
1 teaspoon vanilla extract

1/2 teaspoon brandy extract
6 cinnamon sticks for garnish

Makes 4 servings
Each serving contains:

3/4 milk portion
2 fruit portions
170 calories
11.6 milligrams cholesterol

Put all ingredients except cinnamon sticks in blender and blend until frothy. Pour mixture in a large saucepan and heat until very warm. *Do not boil.* Pour into mugs and garnish with cinnamon sticks.

beverages

CARIBBEAN COOLER

1 small banana, peeled and sliced
1 teaspoon freshly squeezed
   lemon juice
2-1/2 cups pineapple juice
1 cup freshly squeezed orange juice

1 teaspoon vanilla extract
1 teaspoon coconut extract
sugar substitute = 1 teaspoon sugar
1 cup club soda (optional)
mint sprigs for garnish

Makes 8 servings
Each serving contains:
1-1/4 fruit portions
50 calories
0 cholesterol

Put the sliced banana in the blender. Add lemon juice and blend to mix. Put remaining ingredients except club soda and mint in the blender with the banana and blend until frothy. Pour into a large juice container and mix with club soda, if desired. Pour over ice in chilled glasses and garnish with mint sprigs. The soda water makes a lighter, more thirst-quenching drink. The cooler without soda is a smooth brunch drink and is good with rum or vodka for a tall tropical refreshment.

CHI CHI WITH VODKA
CHI CHEATER WITHOUT VODKA

2 cups unsweetened pineapple juice
1-1/2 cups low-fat milk, cold
1/2 cup crushed fresh or canned
   unsweetened pineapple
1 teaspoon vanilla extract

1 teaspoon coconut extract
sugar substitute = 2 teaspoons sugar
1/2 cup crushed ice
vodka (optional)

Makes 6 servings

Each serving contains:
1 fruit portion
1/2 milk portion
80 calories
3.9 milligrams cholesterol

Put all ingredients in blender and blend until frothy. With vodka, add calories depending on the amount and proof. See Alcohol Chart, page 20.

menu planning

There are two one-week menus suggested in this chapter. For these I have selected the two most frequently prescribed calorie levels: 1000 calories per day and 1500 calories per day. Each menu is also limited to 200 milligrams or less of cholesterol per day. Of course, both menus can be used for all calorie levels by slight additions or deletions, once you become more familiar with the diet programs.

A great deal of time and thought on my part has gone into *each* meal for *each* day and for *each* week. I did this so you can use my menu suggestions as party-giving guides for all occasions. I have also added serving suggestions to many of my recipes to further help you with your entertaining. Obviously, *I love* to entertain. I hope I can help you if you like it, too. If you don't, I hope I can inspire you at least to give it a whirl!

The entrées are arranged to give you a variety in taste, types of food and preparation time. However, for maximum time-saving please read the section on Happy Hints carefully. I cannot stress enough the importance of planning ahead to make cooking both more fun and more practical!

Naturally, some of the recipes in this book are more complicated to prepare than you would want to use on a daily basis. However, one of the main purposes of my book is to add interest and variety to family meals and to give you exciting dishes for parties.

Too many people assume that being on a calorie-controlled diet means giving up all of the fun and exotic foods. I tried to disprove this idea with my first book, *The Calculating Cook.* I am making an even greater effort to share with you the excitement of healthful cooking and the delicious results it offers in this book. As before, I want to help you feel better, look younger and live longer.

menu planning

I always chuckle to myself when someone says to me, "I wish I were as slender as you are. Then I could eat anything I wanted." If I really did eat everything I wanted, I wouldn't be thin either!

The word "diet" is perhaps one of the most misused words in the English language. It does not mean something you "go on" and then "go off." According to Webster, diet is "food and drink regularly provided or consumed—habitual course of feeding." In other words, you are literally *always* on a diet. Therefore, developing good eating habits is essential to good health (also essential to a "beautiful" body). And, living on a good diet is made easier when you learn how to *fake* the taste of the *stop*-foods while using only the *go*-foods.

When reading the following menus, please remember you can always substitute a simpler version of the suggested food. For example: If a luncheon menu lists Tuna Soufflé served with Herb Bread and Pear Helena for dessert, you can use the same ingredients with the same number of calories exactly by eating a tuna sandwich, carrot sticks, a pear and a glass of milk—all prepared in about five minutes. My menus are meant to serve as guides for you in learning to prepare your own menus.

So much time is saved by preparing well-planned weekly menus—not only in food preparation but also in shopping. Try to get into the habit of planning your menus two to three weeks in advance. You will be amazed at how much you shorten the amount of time you spend at the market. Also, you will see how many last-minute frustrations are avoided in the kitchen—such as, *no* vanilla for the baked apples or *no* yogurt for the sauce.

Try it, you'll love it!

1000-calorie menus

ONE WEEK MENU

1000 Calories per day
200 Milligrams (or less) Cholesterol per day
Daily Requirements
5 protein
3 fruit
2 starch

1 B vegetable
Group A vegetable as desired*
4 fat
2 milk: non-fat milk
   low-fat milk, subtract
   2 fat from daily allowance
   whole milk, subtract
   4 fat from daily allowance

161

1000-calorie menus

MONDAY/FIRST DAY	Food Group Portion	Calories	Mg. Chol.
BREAKFAST			
1/2 cup fresh orange juice	1 fruit	40	0
liquid egg substitute = 1 egg	1 protein	73	0
1 slice toast	1 starch	68	0
1 teaspoon dietetic jelly	fruit trace	5	0
1-1/4 cups non-fat milk	1-1/4 milk	100	2.9
coffee or tea		0	0
LUNCH			
1 serving Cold Cranberry Soup	1 fruit	40	0
1 serving Party Chicken Platter	2 protein 2 fat	236	50
1 slice Thanksgiving Bread	1 starch	68	2.1
2 slices raw tomato with parsley garnish	*A vegetable	0	0
1 serving Mint Mist	1/2 milk	63	7.7
coffee or tea		0	0
DINNER			
1 serving Celery Root Salad	1 B vegetable 1-1/2 fat	104	5.2
2 slices roast beef (2 ounces)	2 protein	146	62.6
1 serving Ratatouille	1 A vegetable 1/2 fat	23	0
1 serving Pineapple Boats with "Coconut" Sauce	1 fruit 1/4 milk	70	3.9
coffee or tea		0	0

TUESDAY/SECOND DAY	Food Group Portion	Calories	Mg. Chol.
BREAKFAST			
1/2 cup Effie's Baked Applesauce	1 fruit	40	0
3/4 cup non-fat milk on applesauce	3/4 milk	60	1.8
1 serving Breakfast Pizza	1 starch 1/2 fat 1 protein	164	29.1
coffee or tea		0	0
LUNCH			
1/2 serving Marinated Eggplant	1 A vegetable 3/4 fat	34	0
1 serving Bouillabaisse	3 protein 1 fat 1/2 B vegetable	282	54
1 slice crusty French bread	1 starch	68	0
1 serving Prune Mousse	1 fruit 1/4 milk	72	3.9
coffee or tea		0	0
DINNER			
1 serving Cream of Fresh Tomato Soup	1/2 milk 1 fat	85	7.75
raw group A vegetable salad with Sin-Free Salad Dressing	*A vegetable	0 0	0 0
1 serving Broccoli and Cheese Casserole	1-1/2 protein 1/2 fat	132	33.1
1/2 cup Happy Heart Ice Cream	1/2 milk	52	7.7
1 cup strawberries on ice cream	1 fruit	40	0
coffee or tea		0	0

1000-calorie menus

WEDNESDAY/THIRD DAY	Food Group Portion	Calories	Mg. Chol.
BREAKFAST			
1/2 grapefruit	1 fruit	40	0
1 serving Roast Beef Hash	2 protein 1 starch 1 B vegetable	323	60.6
1 cup non-fat milk	1 milk	80	2.3
coffee or tea		0	0
LUNCH			
1 serving Cold Caviar Soup	1/2 protein 1/2 fat	60	97.65
3 slices Melba toast	1/2 starch	34	0
raw celery sticks	*A vegetable	0	0
1 serving Pear Helena with 1/4 cup Helena Sauce	1 fruit 1/2 fat 1/4 milk	75	5
coffee or tea		0	0
DINNER			
lettuce salad with	*A vegetable	0	0
1 tablespoon Happy Heart Italian Dressing	1-1/2 fat	68	0
1 serving Spaghetti Sauce, Bolognese Style	2-1/2 protein 1/2 fat	206	77
1/4 cup spaghetti	1/2 starch	34	0
1 serving Ambrosia	1-1/2 fruit 1/2 milk	123	7.7
coffee or tea		0	0

THURSDAY/FOURTH DAY	Food Group Portion	Calories	Mg. Chol.
BREAKFAST			
2 tablespoons raisins on	1 fruit	108	0
1/2 cup oatmeal mixed with	1 starch		
1/4 cup low-fat cottage cheese and	1 protein	73	0
1/2 cup non-fat milk on top	1/2 milk	40	1.2
coffee or tea		0	0
LUNCH			
1 serving Chef's Salad	2 protein 2-1/4 fat	246	43
1 slice Herb Bread	1 starch 1-1/2 fat	136	0
1/2 cup Happy Heart Ice Cream on	1/2 milk	52	7.7
1/4 cantaloupe	1 fruit	40	0
coffee or tea		0	0
DINNER			
Egg Sprout Soup	*A vegetable	0	0
lettuce and fresh mushroom salad with	*A vegetable	0	0
Sin-Free Salad Dressing		0	0
1 serving Hawaiian Chicken	2 protein 1/2 fruit 1 fat	211	44.8
1/2 cup steamed pea pods	1 B vegetable	36	0
1/2 cup strawberries with	1/2 fruit	20	0
1 cup non-fat milk on top	1 milk	80	2.3
coffee or tea		0	0

1000-calorie menus

FRIDAY/FIFTH DAY	Food Group Portion	Calories	Mg. Chol.
BREAKFAST			
1/2 banana sliced on	1 fruit	40	0
1/4 cup Kellogg's Concentrate with	1 starch	141	0
	1 protein		
1/2 cup low-fat milk on top	1/2 milk	63	7.7
coffee or tea		0	0
LUNCH			
1 serving cold Consommé Madrilene	*A vegetable	0	0
1 serving Tuna Soufflé	2 protein	146	88
1/2 cup fresh fruit compote	1 fruit	40	0
1 cup non-fat milk	1 milk	80	2.3
coffee or tea		0	0
DINNER			
1 serving Happy Heart Caesar Salad	1/4 starch	152	0
	3 fat		
small broiled lamb chop	2 protein	146	56
3/4 small baked potato with chives and	3/4 starch	51	0
2 tablespoons sour cream	1 fat	45	16
1/2 cup steamed carrots with parsley garnish	1 B vegetable	36	0
1 fresh peach, sliced, with	1 fruit	40	0
1/2 cup non-fat milk on top	1/2 milk	40	1.2
coffee or tea		0	0

SATURDAY/SIXTH DAY	Food Group Portion	Calories	Mg. Chol.
BREAKFAST			
2 fresh figs with	1 fruit	40	0
1 cup non-fat milk on top	1 milk	80	2.3
1 slice San Francisco Sourdough French Toast	3/4 protein 1 starch 1/2 fat	146	.7
coffee or tea		0	0
LUNCH			
1/2 serving Taco Salad	1 protein 1 fat	118	30.2
1 hot tortilla (4 triangles)	1 starch	68	0
1 serving Poached Peach Mousse	1 fruit 1/4 milk	103	3.9
coffee or tea		0	0
DINNER			
1 serving Party Fish Platter	3 protein 3 fat	354	54
1 serving Cucumbers Dilly Dilly	1 fat	45	3
1/4 cantaloupe	1 fruit	40	0
1/2 cup non-fat milk	1/2 milk	40	1.2
coffee or tea		0	0

1000-calorie menus

SUNDAY/SEVENTH DAY	Food Group Portion	Calories	Mg. Chol.
BREAKFAST			
1/2 cup grapefruit juice	1 fruit	40	0
1/2 English muffin, toasted, with	1 starch	68	0
1 teaspoon corn oil margarine	1 fat	45	0
1 serving Mushroom Omelet	2 protein	222	2.5
	1 fat		
	1/4 milk		
3/4 cup non-fat milk	3/4 milk	60	1.8
coffee or tea		0	0
LUNCH			
1 serving Greek Salad	1/2 protein	105	3
	1-1/2 fat		
1-1/2 Rye Crisp	1/2 starch	34	0
1/2 cup Effie's Baked Applesauce with	1 fruit	40	0
1/2 cup non-fat milk	1/2 milk	40	1.2
coffee or tea		0	0
DINNER			
1 serving Chicken Veronique	3/4 fat	208	46.7
	2 protein		
	1/4 fruit		
	1/4 starch		
lettuce salad with pineapple and	1 fruit	76	0
1/2 cup shredded carrots with	1 B vegetable		
2 tablespoons Sin-Free Salad Dressing		0	0
1 cup steamed asparagus	1 A vegetable	trace	0
1/4 cup Mystery Pilaf	1/2 starch	34	0
1 serving Mint Mist	1/2 milk	63	7.7
coffee or tea		0	0

1500-calorie menus

ONE WEEK MENU

1500 Calories per day
200 Milligrams (or less) Cholesterol per day
Daily Requirements
6 protein
4 fruit
5 starch

1 B vegetable
Group A vegetable as desired*
8 fat
2 milk: non-fat milk
   low-fat milk, subtract
    2 fat from daily allowance
   whole milk, subtract
    4 fat from daily allowance

1500-calorie menus

MONDAY/FIRST DAY	Food Group Portion	Calories	Mg. Chol.
BREAKFAST			
1/2 grapefruit	1 fruit	40	0
liquid egg substitute = 1 egg, cooked in	1 protein	73	0
1 teaspoon corn oil margarine	1 fat	45	0
1/2 cup Grapenuts with	2 starch	136	0
3/4 cup non-fat milk on top	3/4 milk	60	1.8
coffee or tea		0	0
LUNCH			
1 serving Party Fish Platter	3 protein 3 fat	354	54
1 serving Cucumbers Dilly Dilly	1 fat	45	3
sliced tomatoes	*A vegetable	0	0
1/2 cup Pickled Onion Relish	1 B vegetable	36	0
2 slices Indian Curry Bread	2 starch	136	4.2
1 serving Prune Mousse	1/4 milk 1 fruit	72	1.9
1/2 cup non-fat milk	1/2 milk	40	1.2
coffee or tea		0	0
DINNER			
Egg Sprout Soup	*A vegetable	0	0
1 serving Hawaiian Chicken	2 protein 1/2 fruit 1 fat	211	44.8
1/2 cup Pine Nut Pilaf with raisins	1 starch 1-1/2 fat 1/2 fruit	156	0
1/2 Baked Banana	1 fruit 1/4 fat	51	0
1 serving Mint Mist	1/2 milk	63	7.7
coffee or tea		0	0

TUESDAY/SECOND DAY	Food Group Portion	Calories	Mg. Chol.
BREAKFAST			
1 serving Late-Date Nightcap over	3/4 milk	170	11.6
	2 fruit		
1/2 cup oatmeal	1 starch	68	0
coffee or tea		0	0
LUNCH			
lettuce salad with	*A vegetable	0	0
2 tablespoons Sin-Free Salad Dressing		0	0
1 Monte Cristo Countdown Sandwich	2 starch	445	18
	3 protein		
	2 fat		
3/4 cup Peach Jam	1-1/2 fruit	60	0
1-1/4 cups non-fat milk	1-1/4 milk	100	2.9
coffee or tea		0	0
DINNER			
1 serving Marinated Eggplant with	1 A vegetable	68	0
	1-1/2 fat		
tomatoes and carrot sticks	1/2 B vegetable	18	0
1 serving Bouillabaisse	1/2 B vegetable	282	54
	3 protein		
	1 fat		
1 slice crusty French bread with	1 starch	68	0
1 teaspoon corn oil margarine	1 fat	45	0
1 serving Banana Cream Pie	1 starch	174	2.9
	1-1/2 fat		
	1/4 protein		
	1/2 fruit		
coffee or tea		0	0

1500-calorie menus

WEDNESDAY/THIRD DAY	Food Group Portion	Calories	Mg. Chol.
BREAKFAST			
1/2 cup fresh orange juice	1 fruit	40	0
3 Buttermilk Pancakes	3 starch	204	0
1 teaspoon corn oil margarine	1 fat	45	0
2 slices ham substitute	1 protein	73	0
1/2 cup non-fat milk	1/2 milk	40	1.2
coffee or tea		0	0
LUNCH			
1 serving Taco Salad	2 protein 2 fat	236	60.4
3 Toasted Tortilla Triangles	1/2 starch	34	0
1 small carrot cut in strips	1 B vegetable	36	0
2 servings Pineapple Boats with "Coconut" Sauce	2 fruit 1/2 milk	140	7.8
coffee or tea		0	0
DINNER			
1 serving Astoria Salad	1 fruit 1 fat	85	0
2 servings Broccoli and Cheese Casserole	3 protein 1 fat	266	66.2
1/2 small broiled tomato	1 A vegetable	trace	0
1 slice French Herb Bread	1 starch 1-1/2 fat	136	0
1 serving Chocolate Sundae	1 milk 1/2 fat 1/2 starch	182	15.5
coffee or tea		0	0

THURSDAY/FOURTH DAY	Food Group Portion	Calories	Mg. Chol.
BREAKFAST			
1/2 cantaloupe	2 fruit	80	0
1 serving Breakfast Pizza made with partly skimmed cheese	1 starch 1 protein 1/2 fat	164	18.2
1 cup non-fat milk	1 milk	80	2.3
coffee or tea		0	0
LUNCH			
lettuce salad with 1 tablespoon raisins	1/2 fruit	20	0
2 tablespoons Happy Heart Dressing	4 fat	180	0
1 serving Chicken Curry Soufflé	2 protein 1/4 milk	177	26
2 slices Thanksgiving Bread	2 starch	136	4.2
2 teaspoons corn oil margarine	2 fat	90	0
1/2 cup Effie's Baked Applesauce with	1 fruit	40	0
1/4 cup Rum Custard Sauce	1/4 protein	42	3
coffee or tea		0	0
DINNER			
1 sliced tomato with	1 A vegetable	trace	0
Sin-Free Salad Dressing		0	0
1 serving Braised Lamb Shanks with Mint Sauce	3 protein	219	101
1/2 cup Mystery Pilaf	1 starch 3/4 fat	102	0
1/2 cup steamed carrots	1 B vegetable	36	0
1 serving Old-Fashioned Strawberry Shortcake	1/2 fruit 1 fat 1 starch	133	1.5
3/4 cup non-fat milk	3/4 milk	60	1.8
coffee or tea		0	0

1500-calorie menus

FRIDAY/FIFTH DAY	Food Group Portion	Calories	Mg. Chol.
BREAKFAST			
1 sliced banana on	2 fruit	80	0
1 cup cornflakes with	1-1/2 starch	102	0
1 cup non-fat milk	1 milk	80	2.3
liquid egg substitute = 2 eggs	2 protein	146	0
coffee or tea		0	0
LUNCH			
1 serving Cream of Fresh Tomato Soup	1/2 milk 1 fat	85	7.75

grilled cheese sandwich (2 slices bread,
  2 ounces American Cheese, 2 teaspoons
  corn oil margarine)
	2 starch
	2 protein
	2 fat
		372	56.8

1 cup strawberries with	1 fruit	40	0
1/2 cup non-fat milk on top	1/2 milk	40	1.2
coffee or tea		0	0
DINNER			
1 serving Astoria Salad	1 fruit 1 fat	85	0
1 serving Turkey Provençal with steamed broccoli and	2 protein 1/4 fat 1 B vegetable	193	44.8
1 tablespoon Simple Hollandaise Sauce	2 fat	90	4
1/2 cup noodles	1 starch	68	0
2 Chocolate Mint Drop Cookies	1/2 starch 1-1/2 fat	102	0
coffee or tea		0	0

SATURDAY/SIXTH DAY	Food Group Portion	Calories	Mg. Chol.
BREAKFAST			
1 serving San Francisco Sourdough French Toast	1/2 fat 1 starch 3/4 protein	146	.7
1/2 cup Applesauce Topping	1 fruit	40	0
1-1/2 cups non-fat milk	1-1/2 milk	120	3.5
coffee or tea		0	0
LUNCH			
1 serving Steak Tartare	3 fat 3 protein	354	90.9
2 slices pumpernickel bread	2 starch	136	0
1 teaspoon corn oil margarine	1 fat	45	0
1 cup assorted fresh fruit	2 fruit	80	0
coffee or tea		0	0
DINNER			
lettuce salad with 1/2 cup pineapple and	*A vegetable 1 fruit	40	0
Sin-Free Salad Dressing		0	0
1 serving Dillied Fish Amandine	3 protein 2-1/4 fat	320	60
1/2 cup Mystery Pilaf	1 starch 3/4 fat	102	0
1 serving steamed peas in Onion Cups	1 B vegetable	36	0
1 serving Grasshopper Pie	1/4 milk 1 starch 1-1/2 fat	167	3.9
coffee or tea		0	0

1500-calorie menus

SUNDAY/SEVENTH DAY	Food Group Portion	Calories	Mg. Chol.
BREAKFAST			
3/4 cup orange and grapefruit sections	1-1/2 fruit	60	0
1 serving Mushroom Omelet	2 protein 1 fat 1/4 milk	222	2.5
1 English muffin	2 starch	136	0
2 teaspoons corn oil margarine	2 fat	90	0
1 tablespoon Strawberry Topping (1 cup = 40 calories)	fruit trace	0	0
1 cup non-fat milk	1 milk	80	2.3
coffee or tea		0	0
LUNCH			
Gazpacho Party Mold	*A vegetable	0	0
1 serving Soufflé Olé	2 protein	146	12
6 Toasted Tortilla Triangles	1 starch	68	0
1 serving Pear Helena with Helena Sauce	1 fruit 1/2 fat 1/4 milk	115	5
coffee or tea		0	0
DINNER			
1 serving Asparagus Vinaigrette	1 fat	45	0
1 serving Coq au Vin	2 protein 1 fat 1 B vegetable	227	44.8
1 cup boiled potatoes with	2 starch	136	0
2 teaspoons corn oil margarine	2 fat	90	0
1/2 small broiled tomato	1 A vegetable	trace	0
1 serving Ambrosia	1/2 milk 1-1/2 fruit	123	7.7
coffee or tea		0	0

happy hints

Many of the happiest hints in a cookbook deal with saving time and avoiding last minute preparation problems. Always prepare in advance anything you can. When you are in the kitchen preparing one meal, make use of every spare moment. A beautiful part of saving time by advance preparation is that some sauces are at least three times as good if made in advance.

If you are peeling garlic for one recipe, peel an additional two buds, quarter them and put in one cup of corn oil. I try always to keep garlic-flavored oil on hand for salad dressings and croutons. When chopping onions for one dish, chop enough for anything you plan to make the next day or two. Chopped onions do not freeze well, but can be kept a day or two in the refrigerator in a tightly sealed container.

I use a great deal of parsley for garnish, as well as an ingredient. I keep fresh parsley in a glass of water in the refrigerator. I always keep minced parsley in my freezer. In my opinion, dried parsley tastes exactly like hay smells. If you have a choice between dried parsley and no parsley, no parsley is a far better flavor. Frozen parsley, when thawed, is almost as good as freshly cut parsley.

Many other herbs can also be successfully stored in the freezer: mint, tarragon, cilantro, rosemary and basil to name a few. Just be sure they are kept in tightly sealed containers. When not properly wrapped or sealed, any food will dry out and lose its flavor in the freezer.

Because it is sometimes difficult to find fresh ginger root when you want it, always try to keep it in your freezer. Peel the whole ginger root and grate it, using what you need and putting the remaining ginger in a sealed plastic bag for future use.

happy hints

When possible, prepare more fish, poultry or meat than you are planning to use. Either freeze the entire extra dish to be served for another meal, or chop the leftovers and freeze them in the correct amounts for use in other recipes. I nearly always double my bread recipes and freeze one loaf to have on hand when I want homemade bread and don't have the time to bake it. Spaghetti sauce is another easily doubled recipe that freezes beautifully. It can serve as a delicious spur-of-the-moment entrée for a number of unexpected guests.

When making pancakes, crêpes and waffles, even French toast, make more than you plan to use at the time and freeze what remains. Then, at some future time you can serve your family a fancy breakfast without added morning confusion!

A good time-saving habit in conjunction with your weekly menu planning is a "market morning" or afternoon. This is a once-a-week event when you go to the market with a list of everything you need to prepare the entire week's menu. You can save amazing amounts of money by planning your weekly menus around the market-advertised specials. In this way, you can take full advantage of sale prices. Also, if your market offers discounts on case-buying of staple products you regularly use, you are offered another way to cut the family budget.

After purchasing everything on your list, go home, unpack your groceries and put them away in order of use for the coming week. When storing your fresh vegetables, prepare them for use before putting them in the refrigerator. For example: Wash and dry all of your lettuce and other salad greens such as parsley, spinach, cabbage and watercress. Store them in large plastic bags or in vegetable drawers lined with damp paper towels. Wash vegetables such as potatoes, carrots, squash, cucumbers and tomatoes to save time when you will be ready to peel or chop them. Peel your onions and store them in plastic bags—no more last-minute tears just before a dinner party!

Arrange your spices in alphabetical order. This saves untold amounts of time each week looking for the correct seasonings.

No matter how small your kitchen, establish a pantry (an area where all frequently used ingredients are kept) so that you *never* find yourself out of "something" in the middle of preparing a recipe. In connection with your pantry, keep a pad of paper and pencil in the kitchen as a "control factor." Whenever you open the last bottle, can, jar or box of an item you use regularly, write the item down on the pad to be added to the next week's market shopping list. I refer to such items as coffee, tea, sugar substitutes, salt, spices, extracts, vinegar, cereals, margarine, milk or even plastic bags and aluminum foil.

Use your own imagination as to time that can be saved by advance preparation to avoid undue harassment. Save the time for the things that cannot (or should not) be prepared very much in advance, such as squeezing fresh orange juice, slicing fresh fruit, tossing the salad greens with the dressing, et cetera. A good time saver is to store your stocks in the freezer. Put some of them in one-cup containers and some in ice cube trays for individual servings.

Try to grow at least some of your own herbs if you possibly can. Growing herbs is fun! Fresh herbs add greatly to the flavor of your food and you save time when the fresh herb you need is right outside your back door or on your windowsill.

CURING YOUR SKILLET

You will need non-stick pans for much of your low-fat cooking. Generally, I prefer "cured" heavy iron skillets over Teflon; they are better for browning and I don't have to worry about scratching them.

Take your new iron skillet, or your grandmother's old one, and put several tablespoons of oil in it. Put it on moderate heat and when it starts to get hot, tilt it from side to side until the oil coats the entire inner surface of the skillet. Continue heating the skillet until it gets so hot it starts to smoke. Then, turn the heat off and cool the skillet. When it's cool enough to handle, wipe all the oil out of it with paper towels. Repeat this process three or four times, and you have a "cured" pan.

Never wash a "cured" pan with water. When you are through with it each time, wipe it out with oil. If anything is stuck on the bottom, rub it off with salt. If it is so bad that you have to wash it with water, or if you use it for cooking liquids, all is not lost. Do not throw the pan away because it looks rusty, *just cure it again!*

KITCHEN VOCABULARY

FOR PREPARATION

CHOP Using a large chopping knife, hold point end down with one hand and use the other hand to chop. There are also chopping devices available in most appliance and hardware stores.

COARSELY CHOP Chop in pieces approximately 1/2-inch square.
FINELY CHOP Chop in pieces approximately 1/4-inch square.
MINCE Chop as fine as gravel.
CUBE Cut into cube-shaped pieces approximately 1 inch or specified size.

DICE Cut into 1/4-inch cubes or smaller.
SLICE Using a sharp knife, slice through evenly to specified thickness.
THINLY SLICE Using the slicing side for very thinly sliced vegetables of a 4-sided grater, slice vegetables such as cucumbers and onions.

happy hints

JULIENNE CUT Cut in strips approximately 1/4 inch by 2 inches.

SNIP Cut into small pieces using scissors or kitchen shears.

SCORE Using a knife, make shallow cuts or slits on surface.

SHRED Slice thinly in 2 directions, or use a shredder.

GRATE Rub the surface to be grated on grater for desired-size particles. For example, finely grated and coarsely grated would require 2 different size graters.

GRIND Use a food chopper or grinder.

CRUMBLE Crush with your hands or a fork into crumblings, food such as toast, farmer cheese, et cetera.

PRESS This term applies usually to garlic when using a garlic press.

CRUSH Using a mortar and pestle, crush dry herbs before using.

MASH Potatoes and many other cooked vegetables can be mashed using a potato masher, or brought to the same consistency in an electric blender or mixer.

PEEL Remove outer covering of food such as oranges, lemons and bananas.

PARE Using a knife, remove the outer covering of food such as apples and peaches.

SCRAPE Scrape to remove outer skin on food such as carrots and parsnips, or scrape to produce juice in food such as onions.

SKIN Remove skin of such food as chicken; sometimes used when referring to onions.

CORE Remove core from fruits such as pears and apples.

PIT Remove the pit or seed from fruits such as peaches and plums.

SEED Completely remove small seeds from such foods as tomatoes, cucumbers and bell peppers.

FILLET Remove *all* bones; usually refers to fish.

BONE Remove *all* bones; usually refers to roasts and poultry.

STIR Using a spoon in a circular motion until all ingredients are well mixed.

TOSS Mix from both sides in an under and over motion toward the center, using 2 spoons or a fork and spoon; usually refers to salads.

FOLD IN Using a rubber spatula or spoon in a circular motion coming across the bottom, fold the bottom over the top. Repeat slowly until mixture is folded in as indicated in the recipe.

KNEAD Usually referring to bread dough. After mixing dough according to recipe, place on a floured surface, flatten ball of dough with floured hands and fold it toward you. With the heels of your hands, press down and flatten again. Continue doing this until dough is smooth and satiny, or as recipe directs.

CREAM With a spoon, rub against sides of bowl until creamy. A pastry blender may also be used.

DISSOLVE Mix dry ingredients with liquid until no longer visible in the solution.

WHISK Stir, beat or fold using a wire whisk.

WHIP Beat rapidly with fork, whisk, egg beater or electric mixer to add air and increase volume of mixture.

BEAT Using egg beater or electric mixer, beat to add air and increase volume.

STIFFLY BEATEN Beat until mixture stands in stiff peaks.

STIFF BUT NOT DRY This term is often used for egg whites and means they should hold soft, well-defined peaks but not be beaten to the point where they look as though they will break.

BLEND Combine 2 or more ingredients well; often used when referring to an electric blender.

BLEND UNTIL FROTHY This is a term I use meaning to blend until the volume is almost doubled by the addition of air and is foamy.

PURÉE Put through a fine sieve or food mill, or use an electric blender.

SPRINKLE Just as the word implies, sprinkle, using your fingers as directed in recipe.

DOT Scatter in small bits over surface of food, actually "sprinkling," and usually refers to butter or margarine.

DREDGE Sprinkle lightly with flour, or coat with flour.

COAT Using a sifter, sprinkle ingredient with flour, sugar substitute, et cetera, until coated. Roll in flour or shake in a paper bag until coated.

SIFT Put flour, sugar, et cetera, through a flour sifter or sieve.

GREASE Rub lightly with margarine, corn oil, et cetera.

COOL Allow to stand at room temperature until no longer warm to the touch.

CHILL Place in refrigerator until cold.

MARINATE Allow mixture to stand in marinade for length of time indicated in recipe.

SKEWER Hold together with metal or wooden skewers, or spear chunks of meat/vegetables on wooden skewers, such as for shish kabob.

FOR COOKING

PREHEAT Set oven to desired temperature. Wait until temperature is reached before baking.

BAKE Cook in heated oven.

ROAST To bake meat or poultry.

BROIL Cook under broiler at designated distance.

BARBECUE Cook over hot coals.

TOAST Brown in a toaster, oven or under broiler. When applied to nuts, seeds or coconut, these may be toasted in a 350° oven until desired color is attained. Or, place under broiler and if this method is used watch carefully as they will burn quickly.

BROWN Brown in oven under a broiler or in a heavy iron skillet to desired color.

SEAR Brown surface rapidly over high heat in a hot skillet.

SINGE Usually refers to poultry. Hold over flame to burn off all hairs.

FRY Cook in a small amount of oil in a skillet.

PAN BROIL Cook in ungreased or cured hot skillet pouring off fat as it accumulates.

DEEP FRY Use a deep-fat fryer, adding enough oil to cover food to be cooked. If temperature is given in the recipe, a deep-fat frying thermometer will be needed.

SAUTÉ Cook in small amount of hot oil in a skillet.

BRAISE Brown meat well on all sides, adding a small amount of water or other liquid. Cover and simmer over low heat or place in a moderate oven and cook until tender or as recipe directs.

BOIL Cook food in liquid in which bubbles constantly rise to the surface and break. At sea level, water boils at 212° F.

SIMMER Cook just below boiling point at about 185° F at sea level.

SCALD Heat to just under the boiling point where tiny bubbles start at the side. This is also often called "bring to boiling point."

STEAM To cook food over boiling water using either a steamer or a large kettle with a rack placed in the bottom of it to hold the pan or dish of food above the boiling water.

STEEP Allow to stand in hot liquid.

CODDLE Usually used when referring to eggs. When a raw egg is called for in a recipe such as eggnog, Caesar salad, et cetera, put the egg in boiling water for 30 seconds before using it. The reason for coddling the egg is that avedin, a component of raw egg whites, is believed to block the absorption of biotin, one of the water soluble vitamins. Avedin is extremely sensitive to heat and coddling the egg inactivates the avedin.

PARBOIL Boil in water or other liquid until partially cooked. This is usually done before another form of cooking.

POACH Cook for a short time in simmering liquid.

BLANCH To dip quickly into boiling water. Usually refers to fruits and vegetables. When referring to nuts, cover shelled nuts with cold water and bring to a boil. Remove from heat and drain. Slip skins from nuts.

BASTE Spoon liquid over food while it is cooking as directed, or use a baster.

THICKEN Mix thickening agent, arrowroot, cornstarch, flour, et cetera, with a small amount of the liquid to be thickened and add slowly to the hot liquid, stirring constantly. Cook until slightly thickened or until mixture coats a metal spoon.

FORK TENDER When food can be easily pierced with a fork.

COVER TIGHTLY Sealed so that steam cannot escape.

equivalents

ARTIFICIAL SWEETENERS
(Sugar Substitutes)

Adolph's Sugar Substitute
2 shakes of jar = 1 rounded teaspoon
    sugar
1/4 teaspoon = 1 tablespoon sugar
1 teaspoon = 1/4 cup sugar
2-1/2 teaspoons = 2/3 cup sugar
1 tablespoon = 3/4 cup sugar
4 teaspoons = 1 cup sugar

Sucaryl (Liquid Sweetener)
1/8 teaspoon = 1 teaspoon sugar
1/2 teaspoon = 4 teaspoons sugar
3/4 teaspoon = 2 tablespoons sugar
1-1/2 teaspoons = 1/4 cup sugar
3 teaspoons (1 tablespoon) = 1/2 cup
    sugar
2 tablespoons = 1 cup sugar

Sugar Twin
1 teaspoon = 1 teaspoon sugar

Sugar Twin (brown)
1 teaspoon = 1 teaspoon sugar

Sweet 'N Low
1/10 teaspoon = 1 teaspoon sugar
1/3 teaspoon = 1 tablespoon sugar
1 teaspoon = 1/6 cup sugar
1-1/2 teaspoons = 1/4 cup sugar
3 teaspoons = 1/2 cup sugar
6 teaspoons (2 tablespoons) =
    1 cup sugar

BEVERAGES

Ice cubes
2 ice cubes = 1/4 cup
8 ice cubes = 1 cup

Instant coffee
4-ounce jar = 60 cups coffee

Coffee
1 pound (80 tablespoons) = 40 to
    50 cups

Tea leaves
1 pound = 300 cups tea

FATS

Miscellaneous
Bacon, 1 pound, rendered = 1-1/2 cups
Butter, 1 cube (1/4 pound) = 1/2 cup
    or 8 tablespoons
Cheese, cream, 3-ounce package =
    6 tablespoons
Cream, heavy whipping, 1 cup =
    2 cups, whipped
Margarine, 1 cube (1/4 pound) =
    1/2 cup or 8 tablespoons

Nuts in the shell
Almonds, 1 pound = 1 cup nutmeats
Brazil nuts, 1 pound = 1-1/2 cups
    nutmeats
Peanuts, 1 pound = 2 cups nutmeats
Pecans, 1 pound = 2-1/2 cups nutmeats
Walnuts, 1 pound = 2-1/2 cups
    nutmeats

Nuts, shelled
Almonds, 1/2 pound = 2 cups
Almonds, 42, chopped = 1/2 cup
Brazil nuts, 1/2 pound = 1-1/2 cups

Coconut, 1/2 pound, shredded =
2-1/2 cups
Peanuts, 1/2 pound = 1 cup
Pecans, 1/2 pound = 2 cups
Walnuts, 1/2 pound = 2 cups
Walnuts, 15, chopped = 1/2 cup

FRUITS (DRIED)

Apricots, 24 halves, 1 cup = 1-1/2
cups, cooked
Dates, 1 pound, 2-1/2 cups = 1-3/4
cups, pitted and chopped
Figs, 1 pound, 2-1/2 cups = 4-1/2
cups, cooked
Pears, 1 pound, 3 cups = 5-1/2 cups,
cooked
Prunes, pitted, 1 pound, 2-1/2 cups =
3-3/4 cups, cooked
Raisins, seedless, 1 pound, 2-3/4
cups = 3-3/4 cups, cooked

FRUITS (FRESH)

Apples, 1 pound, 4 small =
3 cups, chopped
Apricots, 1 pound, 6 to 8
average = 2 cups, chopped
Bananas, 1 pound, 4 small =
2 cups, mashed
Berries, 1 pint = 2 cups
Cantaloupe, 2 pounds, 1 average =
3 cups, diced
Cherries, 1 pint = 1 cup, pitted
Cranberries, 1 pound = 4-1/2 cups
Crenshaw melon, 3 pounds, 1 average =
4-1/2 cups, diced
Figs, 1 pound, 4 small = 2 cups,
chopped
Grapefruit, 1 small = 1 cup,
sectioned

Grapes, Concord, 1/4 pound,
30 grapes = 1 cup
Grapes, Thompson seedless,
1/4 pound, 40 grapes = 1 cup
Guavas, 1 pound, 4 medium = 1 cup
chopped
Honeydew melon, 2 pounds, 1 average
= 3 cups, diced
Kumquats, 1 pound, 8 to 10 average =
2 cups, sliced
Lemon, 1 medium (3 average =
1 pound) = 3 tablespoons juice;
2 teaspoons grated peel
Limes, 1/2 pound, 5 average =
4 tablespoons juice; 4 to 5 teaspoons grated peel
Loquats, 1 pound, 5 average =
1-1/2 cups, chopped
Lychees, 1 pound, 6 average =
1/2 cup, chopped
Mangoes, 1 pound, 2 average =
1-1/2 cups, chopped
Nectarines, 1 pound, 3 average =
2 cups, chopped
Orange, 1 small (2 average = 1 pound)
= 6 tablespoons juice; 1 tablespoon
grated peel, 3/4 cup sectioned
Papaya, 1 medium = 1-1/2 cups,
chopped
Peaches, 1 pound, 3 average =
2 cups, chopped
Pears, 1 pound, 3 average = 2 cups,
chopped
Persimmons, 1 pound, 3 average =
2 cups, mashed
Pineapple, 3 pounds, 1 medium =
2-1/2 cups, chopped

Plums, 1 pound, 4 average = 2 cups,
chopped
Pomegranate, 1/4 pound, 1 average =
3 cups seeds
Prunes, 1 pound, 5 average =
2 cups, chopped
Rhubarb, 1 pound, 4 slender stalks =
2 cups, cooked
Tangerines, 1 pound, 4 average =
2 cups, sectioned
Watermelon, 10 to 12 pounds,
1 average = 20 to 24 cups, cubed

HERBS, SPICES AND SEASONINGS

Garlic powder, 1/8 teaspoon =
1 small clove garlic
Ginger, powdered, 1/2 teaspoon =
1 teaspoon, fresh
Herbs, dried, 1/2 teaspoon =
1 tablespoon, fresh
Horseradish, bottled, 2 tablespoons = 1 tablespoon, fresh

MILK

Dry, whole powdered milk, 1/4 cup
+ 1 cup water = 1 cup whole milk
Dry, non-fat powdered milk, 1/3 cup
+ 2/3 cup water = 1 cup non-fat
milk
Skimmed, canned, 1 cup =
5 cups, whipped

PROTEIN

Cheese
Cottage cheese, 1/2 pound = 1 cup
Cheese, grated, 1/4 pound = 1 cup
Eggs and Egg Substitutes
Eggs, raw, whole, 6 medium = 1 cup

equivalents

Eggs, raw, in shell, 10 medium =
1 pound
Egg whites, 1 medium = 1-1/2
tablespoons
Egg whites, 9 medium = 1 cup
Egg yolks, 1 medium = 1 tablespoon
Egg yolks, 16 medium = 1 cup
Egg substitute, liquid, 1/4 cup =
1 egg (see label)
Egg substitute, dry, 3 tablespoons =
1 egg (see label)

Seafood and Fish

Crab, fresh or frozen, cooked or
canned, 1/2 pound (5-1/2- to
7-1/2-ounce tin) = 1 cup
Escargots, 6 snails = 1-1/2 ounces
Lobster, fresh or frozen, cooked,
1/2 pound = 1 cup
Oysters, raw, 1/2 pound = 1 cup
Scallops, fresh or frozen, shucked,
1/2 pound = 1 cup
Shrimp, cooked, 1 pound = 3 cups
Tuna, drained, canned, 6-1/2 to
7 ounces = 3/4 cup

STARCHES

Crumbs

Bread crumbs, soft, 1 slice = 3/4 cup
Bread crumbs, dry, crumbled, 2 slices =
1/2 cup
Bread crumbs, dry, ground, 4 slices =
1/2 cup
Graham crackers, 14 squares, fine
crumbs = 1 cup
Soda crackers, 21 squares, fine
crumbs = 1 cup

Cereals and Noodles

Flour, cake, 1 pound = 4-1/2 cups,
sifted

Flour, all-purpose, 1 pound =
4 cups, sifted
Bulgar, 1/3 cup = 1 cup, cooked
Cornmeal, 1 cup = 4 cups, cooked
Macaroni, 1 pound, 5 cups =
12 cups, cooked
Noodles, 1 pound, 5-1/2 cups =
10 cups, cooked
Oatmeal, quick-cooking, 1 cup =
2 cups, cooked
Spaghetti, 1 pound = 9 cups, cooked

STOCK BASE AND BOUILLON CUBES

Beef Stock Base, Powdered

1 teaspoon = 1 bouillon cube
4 teaspoons + 1-1/4 cups water =
1 10-1/2-ounce can bouillon,
undiluted
1 teaspoon + 5 ounces water =
5 ounces stock
1 teaspoon + 1 cup water =
1 cup bouillon

Chicken Stock Base, Powdered

1 teaspoon = 1 bouillon cube
1 teaspoon + 5 ounces water =
5 ounces stock
1 teaspoon + 1 cup water =
1 cup bouillon

VEGETABLES (DRIED)

Kidney beans, 1 pound, 1-1/2 cups =
9 cups, cooked
Lima or navy beans, 1 pound,
2-1/2 cups = 6 cups, cooked
Rice, 1 pound, 2-1/2 cups =
8 cups, cooked
Split peas, 1 pound, 2 cups =
5 cups, cooked

VEGETABLES (FRESH)

Artichokes, 1/2 pound = 1 average
Asparagus, 1 pound, 18 spears =
2 cups, cut in 1-inch pieces
Avocado, 1 medium = 2 cups, chopped
Beans, green, 1 pound = 3 cups,
chopped and cooked
Beets, 1 pound, medium-size =
2 cups, cooked and sliced
Bell pepper, 1/2 pound, 1 large =
1 cup, seeded and finely chopped
Broccoli, 1 pound, 2 stalks = 6 cups,
chopped and cooked
Brussels sprouts, 1 pound, 28 average =
4 cups
Cabbage, 1 pound = 4 cups, shredded;
2-1/2 cups, cooked
Carrots, 1 pound, 8 small = 4 cups,
chopped
Cauliflower, 1-1/2 pounds, 1 average =
6 cups, chopped and cooked
Celery, 1 stalk = 1/2 cup, finely
chopped
Celery root, 1-3/4 pounds, 1 average =
4 cups raw, grated; 2 cups,
cooked and mashed
Corn, 6 ears = 1-1/2 cups, cut
Cucumber, 1 medium = 1-1/2 cups, sliced
Eggplant, 1 pound, 1 medium =
12 1/4-inch slices; 6 cups, cubed
Lettuce, 1 average head = 6 cups,
bite-size pieces
Lima beans, baby, 1 pound = 2 cups
Mushrooms, fresh, 1/2 pound,
20 medium = 2 cups raw, sliced
Okra, 24 medium = 1/2 pound
Onion, 1 medium = 1 cup, finely
chopped

Parsnips, 1 pound, 6 average =
4 cups, chopped

Peas, in pods, 1 pound = 1 cup,
shelled and cooked

Pimiento, 1 4-ounce jar = 1/2 cup,
chopped

Potatoes, 1 pound, 4 medium =
2-1/2 cups, cooked and diced

Pumpkin, 3 pounds, 1 average piece =
4 cups, cooked and mashed

Rutabagas, 1-1/2 pounds, 3 small =
2 cups, cooked and mashed

Spinach, 1 pound = 8 cups, uncooked;
2 cups, cooked

Squash, acorn, 1-1/2 pounds, 1 average
= 2 cups, cooked and mashed

Squash, banana, 3 pounds, 1 average
piece = 4 cups, cooked and mashed

Squash, summer, 1 pound, 4 average =
1 cup, cooked

Squash, zucchini, 1 pound, 2 average =
1-1/4 cups, cooked and chopped;
3 cups raw, diced

Tomatoes, 1 pound, 3 medium =
1-1/4 cups, cooked and chopped

Turnips, white, 1 pound, 3 small =
2 cups, peeled and grated;
1-1/4 cups, cooked and mashed

MISCELLANEOUS

Chocolate, 1 square, 1 ounce =
4 tablespoons, grated

Gelatin, sheet, 4 sheets = 1 envelope

Gelatin, powdered, 1/4-ounce envelope
= 1 scant tablespoon

Yeast, fresh, 1 package = 2 tablespoons

Yeast, dry, 1 envelope (to be recon-
stituted in 2 tablespoons water) =
1-3/4 tablespoons

WEIGHTS AND MEASURES AND CAN SIZES

SPOON Fill to slightly overflowing and pass straight edge of knife over spoon to make certain it is *exactly* level.

CUP If cup is even, fill to slightly overflowing and run a straight edge over top to level off. If measuring to a line in the cup, hold cup up to the light to make certain top leveling of dry or liquid ingredient is exactly even.

FAT A simplified method of measuring fat is with water. For example, to measure 1/4 cup of margarine, fill a cup to 3/4 measure with water and add margarine until water level reaches 1 cup.

PINCH What you can hold between thumb and forefinger. I don't like this term for measuring and never use it in my own recipes because the size of the hand makes too much difference. I use the term dash.

DASH Less than 1/8 teaspoon.

3 teaspoons = 1 tablespoon
4 tablespoons = 1/4 cup
8 tablespoons = 1/2 cup
16 tablespoons = 1 cup
2 cups = 1 pint
4 cups = 1 quart

CAN SIZES AND APPROXIMATE YIELD

6-1/2-ounce can tuna = 3/4 cup

7-1/2- to 8-ounce can shrimp, salmon, pimiento = 1 cup

No. 1 can, short or small, 10 to 13 ounces canned soup = 1-3/4 cups

No. 303 can, 16 to 17 ounces = 2 cups

No. 1 can, tall or square, 1 pound salmon, asparagus tips = 2 cups

No. 2 can, 1 pound 4 ounces vegetables such as corn and beans; some fruit = 2-1/2 to 3 cups

No. 2-1/2 can, 1 pound 12 ounces = 4-1/2 cups

No. 3 can, 51 ounces or 46 fluid ounces = 5-3/4 cups

METRIC WEIGHTS

For Dry Measure

Convert known ounces into grams by multiplying by 28

Convert known pounds into kilograms by multiplying by .45

Convert known grams into ounces by multiplying by .035

Convert known kilograms into pounds by multiplying by 2.2

For Liquid Measure

Convert known ounces into milli-liters by multiplying by 30

Convert known pints into liters by multiplying by .47

Convert known quarts into liters by multiplying by .95

Convert known gallons into liters by multiplying by 3.8

Convert known milliliters into ounces by multiplying by .034

bibliography

Bowes & Church. *Food Values of Portions Commonly Used* (11th edition). Philadelphia: J. B. Lippincott Company, 1970.

Chef Gregoire. *Techniques of French Cuisine.* Los Angeles: Le Gourmet French Cooking School, 1967.

Cheraskin, M.D., D.M.D., H., W.M. Ringsdorf, Jr., D.M.D., M.S. and J.W. Clark, D.D.S. *Diet and Disease.* Emmaus, Pennsylvania: Rodale Press, 1968.

Ellenberg, M.D., Max, and Harold Rifkin, M.D. *Diabetes Mellitus: Theory & Practice.* New York: McGraw Hill, 1970.

Eshleman, Ruthe, and Mary Winston. *The American Heart Association Cookbook.* New York: David McKay Company, Inc., 1973.

Feely, R.M., P.E. Cainer and B.K. Watt. "Cholesterol Content of Foods," *Journal of the American Dietetic Association,* Vol. LXI (August, 1972), 134-148.

Jones, Jeanne. *The Calculating Cook.* San Francisco: 101 Productions, 1972.

Taylor, Eileen, and Jacqueline Sooter. *Cholesterol and Fatty Acid Composition of Foods.* San Diego: The Lipid Research Clinic, University of California, 1973.

"Composition of Foods—Raw, Processed, Prepared," *Revised U.S.D.A. Agricultural Handbook,* Number 8, 1973.

index

index

index

biographical notes

JEANNE JONES

In her cookbooks Jeanne Jones combines a creative talent for gourmet cooking and an international background in the study of foods with a sound knowledge of nutrition and its practical application. Jeanne Jones is a diabetic, but after her diagnosis refused to relinquish her role as cook and hostess and devoted herself to the study of nutrition and research into the diabetic diet. With the help of dietitians, she translated into the diet program her recipes collected during her worldwide travels. This was the basis of her first book, *The Calculating Cook,* published in 1972 by 101 Productions. Subsequently the book has been approved for use by diabetics by the American Diabetes Association and won first place as the best adult book of the year in a writing contest sponsored by the National Federation of Press Women.

Shortly after publication of *The Calculating Cook,* Jeanne's husband, newspaper executive Robert Letts Jones, was told by his doctor that he had to bring his cholesterol count down. Six months later, his cholesterol count had dropped to an acceptable level. Realizing that her diabetic diet was beneficial to his cholesterol problems, she started writing *Diet for a Happy Heart,* basing her recipes on the healthful diabetic diet and keeping cholesterol as low as possible. Again she worked closely with doctors and dietitians in researching this book.

In addition to her writing, raising two sons and extensive entertaining, Jeanne Jones devotes herself to helping other diabetics through work with the American Diabetes Association. She is a member of the editorial board of *Diabetes Forecast* and a member of the Board of Directors of the San Diego County Heart Association, affiliated with both the American Heart Association and the California Heart Association.

JEREMIAH

Jeremiah Goodman is a New Yorker whose design and illustration commissions have taken him all over the world with work in a presidential palace in Africa, a gambling casino in Lebanon, an Italian industrialist's penthouse office in Paris and the Gracie Square mansion in New York. He has been a Lord & Taylor illustrator for many years and created the drawings for Dorothy Rodger's book, *My Favorite Things.* Jeremiah has a special interest in the subject matter of *Diet for a Happy Heart:* He describes himself as "A survivor of an exciting heart attack that I consider a rewarding experience."